WHAT ARE THEY SAYING ABOUT
THE CATHOLIC EPISTLES?

What Are They Saying About the Catholic Epistles?

Philip B. Harner

PAULIST PRESS
New York/Mahwah, N.J.

Cover design by Jim Brisson

Library of Congress Cataloging-in-Publication Data

Harner, Philip B.
    What are they saying about the Catholic Epistles? / Philip B. Harner.
      p. cm.
    Includes bibliographical references.
    ISBN 0-8091-4188-4 (alk. paper)
    1. Bible. N.T. Catholic Epistles—Criticism, interpretation, etc. I. Title.
BS2777.H37 2004
227'.906—dc22

2004003380

Published by Paulist Press
997 Macarthur Boulevard
Mahwah, New Jersey 07430

www.paulistpress.com

Printed and bound in the
United States of America

Contents

*To the Students and Faculty
of the Department of Religion
Heidelberg College
1962–1997*

Abbreviations

AB	Anchor Bible
ABD	Anchor Bible Dictionary
ACNT	Augsburg Commentary on the New Testament
AnBib	Analecta biblica
ASNU	Acta seminarii neotestamentici Upsaliensis
BZNW	Beihefte zur Zeitschrift fuer die neutestamentliche Wissenschaft
CBQ	Catholic Biblical Quarterly
DSBS	Daily Study Bible Series
HNT	Handbuch zum Neuen Testament
HTKNT	Herders theologischer Kommentar zum Neuen Testament
IB	Interpreter's Bible
IBC	Interpreter's Bible Commentary
IDB	Interpreter's Dictionary of the Bible
Int	Interpretation
IOVCB	Interpreter's One-Volume Commentary on the Bible
JBC	Jerome Biblical Commentary
JBL	Journal of Biblical Literature
JR	Journal of Religion
JTS	Journal of Theological Studies
NABPRSSS	National Association of the Baptist Professors of Religion Special Study Series

NCE	New Catholic Encyclopedia
NIB	New Interpreter's Bible
NIGTC	New International Greek Testament Commentary
NIVAC	New International Version Application Commentary
NovT	Novum Testamentum
NTM	New Testament Message
NTS	New Testament Studies
PNTC	Pillar New Testament Commentary
RVV	Religionsgeschichtliche Versuche und Vorarbeiten
SBLMS	Society of Biblical Literature Monograph Series
WBC	Word Biblical Commentary
WUNT	Wissenschaftliche Untersuchungen zum Neuen Testament
ZNW	Zeitschrift fuer die neutestamentliche Wissenschaft
ZTK	Zeitschrift fuer Theologie und Kirche

Introduction

This book seeks to survey recent study of the letters of James; 1 and 2 Peter; 1, 2, and 3 John; and Jude. These letters are known collectively as the Catholic or General Epistles, on the grounds that they were originally addressed to early Christians in general. In this respect, the Catholic Epistles differ from the letters of Paul, for example, which were usually addressed to specific churches, such as those in Corinth or Rome.

Robert L. Webb notes that some writers of the late second and third centuries used the term "catholic" to describe an individual epistle. For example, Apollonius (died about 184 CE) used it to designate a letter written by the heretic Themiso. Clement of Alexandria (died 215 CE) applied it to the letter arising from the Council of Jerusalem in Acts 15:22–29. Origen, in the first half of the third century, applied the term to 1 John, 1 Peter, and the *Epistle of Barnabas.*[1]

This early use of the term, Webb suggests, probably arose from the theological use of "catholic" to designate the universal church in contrast to a local congregation. The phrase "catholic epistle" thus signified an encyclical letter, written to a wider, more general audience of early Christians.[2]

In the fourth century the phrase "Catholic Epistles" came into use to designate the seven New Testament writings as a collection. Eusebius (died about 340 CE) and Athanasius (died about 373 CE) used it in this sense. Webb suggests that several factors facilitated the use of "Catholic Epistles" in this sense—the use of "catholic" to describe a general letter, the application of the term to 1 John and 1 Peter, and the collection of the letters of Paul.[3]

Raymond E. Brown notes that in the East, the expression "Catholic Epistles" was generally understood to mean that these seven letters were addressed to groups of Christians in various places or to Christians in general. This designation, he comments, was not entirely appropriate, since 1 Peter was addressed to specific churches, 2 John to an individual church, and 3 John to an individual person.[4]

Brown also notes that there was another interpretation in the West of "catholic, universal." Here the term referred to the general acceptance of these epistles in the church. The Catholic Epistles, therefore, were sometimes known as *epistulae canonicae,* or canonical epistles.[5]

Brown also mentions a point that applies to the study of any New Testament writing. He notes that titles indicating authorship were prefixed to New Testament books only toward the end of the second century. These titles, he suggests, represented the beliefs about authorship held by Christian scholars of that period. These beliefs were intelligent guesses but not necessarily correct.[6] It follows that study of a New Testament writing today may, and should, be willing to examine the question of authorship.

In her recent commentary, Pheme Perkins calls attention to the slow acceptance of some of the Catholic Epistles into the early church's canon. Apart from 1 Peter and 1 John, she notes, these letters "belonged to the disputed 'edges' of the canon" until the end of the fourth century.[7] Perkins also raises the question how widely they are known today, pointing out that the *Revised Common Lectionary* has relatively few selections from 1 Peter, James, Jude, or 2 Peter.[8] Her comment focuses on an issue of concern to many Christians today.

This study provides a survey of scholarship on the Catholic Epistles from approximately 1950 to 2000, with emphasis on the latter part of this period. It addresses issues such as authorship and date, sources and affinities, literary genre and structure, setting and purpose, and Christological and theological formulations. Wherever possible, the study points out areas of consensus or specific trends in the interpretation of the individual epistles.

For technical reasons it was necessary to omit macrons and other diacritical marks in the transliteration of Greek words. Readers with a knowledge of Greek should be able, however, to identify the words without difficulty.

Occasionally I have included translations of brief passages from modern authors in languages other than English. The translations are my own, but I have always provided references so that readers may consult the original if they wish.

It is my hope that this book may contribute to an awareness of recent scholarship, a greater understanding of the Catholic Epistles, and a deeper appreciation for their rich contribution to Christian faith and life.

—*Philip B. Harner*
Professor of Religion, Emeritus
Heidelberg College

1
James

Recent interpretations of the letter of James address issues of authorship and date, sources and affinities, occasion and setting, genre and structure, faith and works, and major characteristics and concerns. In some cases it is possible to identify specific trends or broad areas of agreement. In other instances it is possible to describe only the variety of interpretations that recent scholars have proposed.

Authorship and Date

The "traditional" view, as it may be called, is that James the brother of Jesus wrote the letter of James. Among modern scholars, **Franz Mussner** argues cogently for this view. He points especially to the letter's synthesis of faith and works, in opposition to Paul's "law-free" gospel. James, he argues, is concerned with a synthesis of faith and works that *as such* presupposes the polemical alternative of faith versus works. This alternative became explicable only when the un-Jewish separation of faith and works became explicit—that is, it presupposes the preaching of Paul.[1]

In Mussner's view, the letter of James belongs to a period, perhaps soon after the letter to the Romans or about 60 CE, when this discussion concerning faith and works was a living issue. James, however, evidently does not know the letters of Paul themselves. The fact that he makes no reference to these letters is a decisive objection to the late dating of the letter.[2]

Mussner also cites two other factors indicating traditional authorship and an early date for James. After the year 70, he believes, there was no longer any representative Jewish Christianity within the church and outside of Palestine that could be identified with the "twelve tribes of the Dispersion" to which the letter is sent. Further, James makes no allusion to the special situation of Jewish Christian communities, such as legal and cultic issues, which arose after the catastrophe of 70 CE. Both these factors, Mussner holds, indicate that the letter must have been written before 70 CE.[3]

From a different point of view, Mussner rejects an anti-Gnostic explanation that would entail a second-century date for James. This view holds that James borrowed Gnostic terminology such as "implanted word" (1:21) and "perfect" (1:25) and then used it against Gnostic opponents. Mussner rejects this argument on the grounds that these terms do not occur in polemical contexts, but polemical passages, in contrast, do not use them.[4]

George Eldon Ladd also supports the traditional view that James the brother of Jesus wrote the letter. The major objection to this view, he believes, is that the letter makes no clear reference to Jesus and his teaching. Ladd considers it a "psychologically sound principle," however, that James might have chosen to downplay the fact that he was the brother of Jesus.[5] Ladd also emphasizes that the hope for an imminent return of the Lord (5:7–9) argues for an early date.[6]

Peter H. Davids approaches the question of authorship in relation to his view of the letter as a work that was produced in two stages. He believes that James the brother of Jesus could have been the author of materials (homilies, sayings, and maxims) belonging to the first stage. James might also have been the editor-author of the second stage, putting his own homilies together into epistolary form, possibly assisted at this point by an amanuensis with considerable ability in literary Greek.[7]

Davids argues further that the use of a preliterary tradition of the teachings of Jesus and the absence of references to the inclusion of Gentiles suggest that James the brother of Jesus may have produced the letter between the year 40 CE and the Jerusalem Council. The later redaction of the letter probably took place in a Jewish Christian setting between 55 and 65, or possibly 75 and 85, CE.[8]

With a similar emphasis on the role of oral communication, **Cain Hope Felder** suggests that the original text of the letter was a sermon by James the brother of Jesus in the months prior to his martyrdom in Jerusalem. Then a redactor edited this sermon, giving it the style of an encyclical, in the late 80s or 90s. This redactor was also skilled in writing Hellenistic Greek.[9]

Another recent commentator, **Luke Timothy Johnson,** believes that James the brother of Jesus is "the best candidate" for the role of author. There is no reason, he argues, to suppose that the section on faith and works (2:14–26) must presuppose Paul's teaching in Galatians and Romans and must therefore be later than these writings. James and Paul, he holds, were dealing with different situations.[10]

From another perspective, **Douglas J. Moo** finds support for the traditional view of authorship by referring to the role of James of Jerusalem in the book of Acts. He believes that the letter of James has some similarities to the speech that James of Jerusalem gave to the Apostolic Council (Acts 15:13–21) and to the letter that he sent to the Gentiles in northern Syria and southern Asia Minor (Acts 15:23–29). Moo also believes that the circumstances reflected in the letter fit the situation in which James of Jerusalem would be writing — that is, Jewish Christians, as a result of persecution, have left their homes in Palestine (cf. Acts 11:19) and are now relocating and facing economic distress.

One objection to the traditional view of authorship, Moo notes, is that James of Jerusalem would not write such a "liberal" letter addressing ethical aspects of Jewish law but ignoring ritual issues such as food laws and purification rites. Moo argues, however, that James is presumably silent about the ritual law because it is not an issue in the communities to which he is writing.[11]

As this survey indicates, those who support the traditional view of authorship refer to issues such as faith and works, the relation of James to Paul's letters, the question of Gnosticism, references to Jesus' teachings, the process by which the letter was produced, the quality of the Greek, and the absence of ritual issues. It is interesting that many interpreters who question the traditional view address some of these same topics but see them from a different perspective. These interpreters represent the position that a later, anonymous author was responsible for the letter of James.

Near the beginning of the period covered by this book, **Burton Scott Easton** described three difficulties with the traditional view that James the brother of Jesus wrote the letter. This James, first of all, must have been thoroughly familiar with Jesus and his teachings. Yet the letter of James cites no saying of Jesus directly, and very few indirectly. No book in the New Testament, Easton believes, tells us less about Jesus.

A second difficulty, Easton believes, concerns the writer's use of literary forms and sources. He employs the Hellenistic, non-Semitic forms of prose paraenesis (ethical exhortation) and diatribe (debate with an imaginary opponent); he reflects familiarity with Stoic-Cynic ethical terminology; and in 4:6, he cites the Old Testament (Prov 3:34) from the Septuagint translation rather than the Hebrew text. James the brother of Jesus would not be expected to make use of forms and sources such as these.

The third difficulty concerns the writer's attitude toward the law. James the brother of Jesus would have advocated the type of Jewish Christianity represented in Acts 21:20–25, which drew a sharp distinction between Jewish and Gentile believers. The former were "all zealous for the law," including the moral and ceremonial laws. The writer of the letter of James, however, gives no hint of two classes of Christians and shows no interest at all in the ceremonial laws.

For these reasons Easton thinks that some later writer attributed the letter to James as a respected figure of the early church, much as other anonymous writers used the name *Peter* at the beginning of 2 Peter or *Paul* at the beginning of the Pastoral Epistles.[12]

In developing his interpretation of the letter, Easton — virtually alone among modern scholars — refers sympathetically to a theory that **Arnold Meyer** published in 1930. Meyer held that the letter of James, which arose perhaps in 80–90 CE, was a slightly modified version of an allegorical Jewish writing, "The Letter of Jacob to the Twelve Tribes." This Jewish source was produced in the Hellenistic synagogues, perhaps in the area between Antioch and Caesarea, about the time of Philo. In this allegory, by analogy with Genesis 49, the patriarch Jacob addressed each of the Twelve Tribes in the Diaspora of Hellenistic Judaism.[13]

Meyer believed that this Jewish document provided the basis for the letter of James in the New Testament. "The essential content of the letter of James," he wrote, "is Jewish material; it nowhere reveals a Christian spirit or specifically Christian forms of expression."[14] A later editor made several Christian additions to this Jewish original, such as the mention of Christ (1:1; 2:1) and the church (5:14), and possibly the Christian form of the prohibition against swearing (5:12).[15]

Easton considers it a "very attractive hypothesis" that this Jewish source underlies the letter of James.[16] He believes, however, that the Christian editor contributed more than the minimal additions that Meyer identified. The editor, for example, was wholly responsible for the discussion of faith and works in 2:14–26. This editor, Easton believes, produced the letter of James between 80 and 100 CE.[17]

Albert E. Barnett addresses the question of authorship with reference to canonicity. Authorship by James the brother of Jesus is unlikely, he argues, because prior to Origen the letter was unknown outside its place of origin and thereafter it was accepted slowly in Syria and the West. Apostolicity early became a criterion

for canonicity, and the slowness with which James won acceptance reflects skepticism about its authorship.[18]

In his 1964 commentary, **Bo Reicke** places James—along
with 2 Peter, Jude, and *1 Clement*—in the setting of the social and
political conditions toward the close of the reign of the emperor
Domitian (81–96 CE). All four writings, he believes, were composed in approximately the same period. All four emphasize that
Christians should cultivate a cooperative attitude toward the state
and society if they are to be successful in promoting the gospel.[19]

The letter of James, Reicke believes, is not concerned with
problems of the Jerusalem church but with persecutions by Gentiles, relations with secular powers, and other problems of Christian congregations in the Greco-Roman world. A later writer,
possibly a disciple of James the brother of Jesus, wrote the letter
about 90 CE.[20]

Like Barnett, **Richard L. Scheef Jr.** points out that James
was apparently not known in early Christian churches until the
time of Origen at the close of the second century. This strongly
suggests, he believes, that someone other than James the brother
of Jesus wrote the letter. Scheef also notes that the writer uses
excellent Greek, which would not be expected in an Aramaic-
speaking Jew of Jerusalem. Scheef dates the composition of
James about 100–125 CE, some years after the collection of
Paul's letters about 95 CE.[21]

Since James the brother of Jesus was known for his legalism
and ritualism, **Martin Dibelius** denies that this James could have
written the letter. The writer does speak of fulfilling the entire law
(2:10), but he does not apply this advice to major issues of concern in Judaism, such as Sabbath observance, circumcision, and
purification laws. The fact that the author speaks of the "law of
liberty" (1:25; 2:12) indicates that he is not thinking of the
Mosaic law. The writer enjoins purity from the world (1:17) but
does not touch on difficult problems, such as food laws, that were
associated with this idea at the time of Jesus.

Dibelius believes that a later writer, one of the "teachers" mentioned in 3:1, produced the letter of James. The fact that healing through prayer, originally a pneumatic occurrence, has been transferred to church officials in 5:14 points to a second or third Christian generation as an approximate date. Dibelius notes, however, that the traditional and timeless character of paraenesis cautions against a precise dating.[22]

R. A. Martin offers a compromise view of authorship, arguing that James of Jerusalem probably did not write the letter but suggesting that he might have been the source for some of its material.

Martin gives three main reasons for denying that James the brother of Jesus wrote the letter—the author does not identify himself as the Lord's brother or refer to the life and ministry of Jesus; James the brother of Jesus, as an Aramaic-speaking Jewish Christian, would probably not have written such polished, literary Greek; the letter must be subsequent to Paul's ministry, since it addresses a misunderstanding of his teaching on faith and works.

Martin concludes that the letter of James was probably written toward the end of the first century by "a Hellenistic Christian of the Jewish Christian, non-Pauline church outside Palestine." He also suggests that some of the material in the letter may indeed have come from James of Jerusalem, who died about 62 CE.[23]

Sophie Laws calls attention to the fact that the letter of James discusses faith and works (2:14–26) without specific reference to "works of the law." Of the various arguments against the traditional view of authorship, she regards this as "the most telling." James of Jerusalem, who knew Paul personally and was loyal to the Jewish law, would have appreciated the Pauline debate concerning the role of the law in salvation.

Although the letter of James is often characterized as a document of Jewish Christianity, Laws questions whether the author and his readers were actually Jewish Christians. The author, for example, upholds the Jewish law (1:25; 2:10, 12) but refers only to the Decalogue (2:11) and the love commandment of Leviticus

19:18 (2:8). He shows no interest in observances (Sabbath, food laws, circumcision) that served to preserve Jewish identity in the Hellenistic world. He does not appreciate that the faith-works controversy had any implications for the Jewish law.

For these reasons Laws believes that the background of the author and his readers probably lies among the "God-fearers," that is, non-Jews who respected the monotheism and ethics of Judaism but did not become proselytes. These people evidently formed a receptive audience for Christian preaching. Whenever they became Christian, they would bring their knowledge of Judaism with them into their new faith.[24]

In her recent commentary, **Pheme Perkins** argues that the author of James appears to be a Greek-speaking Jewish Christian rather than James the brother of the Lord. She believes, for example, that a Galilean craftsman could not produce the polished Greek style of the letter. She notes that the requirements of the law are formulated in Hellenistic Jewish terms, without any discussion of ritual requirements. Perkins observes, finally, that the style of exhortation follows conventions of Hellenistic rhetoric, such as the diatribe.[25]

Regarding the authorship and date of James, it does not appear possible to identify trends of interpretation or broad areas of agreement. Supporters of traditional and non-traditional views tend to address many of the same issues, such as faith and works, references to Jesus and his teaching, the literary quality of the Greek, and the understanding of Jewish law. This survey does illustrate how the question of authorship and date is closely related to other issues, such as the letter's literary sources, the role of oral communication, the social and political setting, and the relation to Paul and his letters.

Sources and Affinities

Interpreters of James offer several views of its literary sources and affinities. Some emphasize the Hellenistic or Greco-Roman background. Others understand the letter in relation to the

Judeo-Christian tradition—the Old Testament, Judaism, the teaching of Jesus, or early Christian writings. Many interpreters think in terms of multiple sources or parallels.

As it was noted above, **Burton Scott Easton** subscribes to the theory of **Arnold Meyer** that a Jewish document, "The Letter of Jacob to the Twelve Tribes," underlies major portions of the letter of James. In developing this source, the Christian editor contributed the discussion of faith and works in 2:14–26. He also utilized a separate Jewish source in 2:1–13, concerning rich men in the synagogues, and he drew on Stoic-Cynic material for the section on sins of the tongue in 3:1–12.

Easton also emphasizes that the editor's rhetorical training was Hellenistic. He utilized the literary form of paraenesis, frequently along with the diatribe. Both these forms, Easton believes, were Hellenistic. Thus the Christian editor of James employed a Jewish document as his basic source but developed it in terms of his Hellenistic rhetorical training.[26]

Jean Cantinat also regards paraenesis as the predominant literary genre in James, but he thinks in terms of broader sources and parallels. He describes the exhortations in James as analogous to those of all the moralists of the time. In particular, he mentions those of the wisdom literature of the Bible (e.g., Proverbs and Sirach) and the "pagan masters of the diatribe" (Zeno, Seneca, and Epictetus).[27]

Even more broadly, **Sophie Laws** finds many allusions in James to Hellenistic life and culture. These include references to popular philosophy (1:21; 3:6), Greek and Latin literature (3:3–4, 7; 4:14), astronomy (1:17), popular superstition (4:15), and magic (2:19; 4:7).[28] These allusions suggest that the author of James—whoever he was—clearly had some familiarity with the popular Hellenistic culture of his time.

Scholars also interpret James in relation to its background in the Old Testament, Judaism, Jesus' teachings, and early Christianity. **Franz Mussner,** for example, emphasizes the ideal of the "piety of the poor." "There is scarcely an element of the Old

Testament and late Jewish piety of the poor," he writes, "that does not occur also in the letter of James." Similarly, he finds close connections between this type of piety in James and the preaching of Jesus.[29]

Luke Timothy Johnson suggests that James reflects the perspective of the Old Testament prophets in understanding human life as covenantal and relational. He also believes that James represents the wisdom tradition of the Old Testament, not only in using proverbs and maxims, but also in presenting human freedom as the choice between "wisdom from above" and "wisdom from below" (1:5; 3:13–18). Johnson also emphasizes that James has a positive view of the Jewish law, understood as moral commandment rather than ritual obligation.[30]

In contrast to those who emphasize the wisdom tradition in James, **Douglas J. Moo** argues that the theme of wisdom is not central to the letter as a whole. He notes that James has only two actual references to wisdom (1:5 and 3:13–18), and he holds that wisdom is not the real topic in either passage. He argues also that only a small part of James consists of the brief "proverbs" familiar from wisdom literature. While wisdom has some place in James's theology, Moo concludes that it lacks a central, integrative role.[31]

Interpreters have differed in their understanding of the relation between James and the teaching of Jesus. In his 1957 commentary, **Burton Scott Easton** was reluctant to think of the teaching of Jesus as a source for the content and theology of the letter of James. No book in the New Testament, he held, tells us less about Jesus.[32] Like Arnold Meyer before him, Easton saw James as essentially a Jewish writing with occasional Christian additions.

Subsequent interpreters have been more inclined to find parallels to the teachings of Jesus. **Sophie Laws** argues, for example, that James' prohibition of oaths (5:12) clearly recalls Jesus' prohibition (Matt 5:33–37). James speaks of the commandment of love for neighbor (Lev 19:18) as the "royal law" (2:8), calling attention to this commandment just as Jesus did (Mark 12:31). James' encouragement to "ask...and it will be given" (1:5) recalls Jesus' instruction to do so (Matt 5:7–11; Luke 11:9–13), and his description of the poor as "heirs of the kingdom" (2:5) recalls Jesus' beatitude on the poor (Matt 5:3; Luke 6:20).[33]

Many recent interpreters find echoes in James of the Sermon on the Mount (Matt 5–7), along with some other teachings of Jesus. "No other book in the New Testament," Cantinat writes, "offers as many echoes of this Sermon as the letter of James."[34] In a similar way Mussner concludes, "To listen to James, therefore, is to listen to Jesus!"[35]

Interpreters such as Dibelius, Davids, Laws, and Johnson believe that James was in contact with a continuing oral tradition. He was evidently familiar with some sayings of Jesus as they existed at a preliterary stage, before their incorporation into the synoptic gospels and their fixation in written form. Davids, in particular, suggests that these contacts with the preliterary synoptic tradition support an early date for the letter and authorship by James the brother of Jesus.[36]

Some interpreters also believe that James reflects an awareness of early Christian ritual and catechesis. **Bo Reicke** finds a reference to baptism in 1:18, combined with the idea of first fruits as an offering to God (Deut 26:1–11). He also understands the "implanted word" in 1:21 as a reference to baptism.[37] **Thomas W. Leahy** believes that 1:2–3, 12 may reflect dependence on an early Christian hymn, perhaps from the baptismal liturgy. He also thinks that 1:18, 21 may reflect a baptismal liturgy.[38]

Sophie Laws argues that the allusion to God as the one who "brought us forth by the word of truth" (1:18 [RSV]) probably expresses the idea of rebirth—that is, conversion and baptism. She believes also that parallels between James and 1 Peter may reflect a common pattern of early Christian catechetical teaching (Jas 1:2–4 and 1 Pet 1:6–7; Jas 1:18, 21 and 1 Pet 1:23—2:2; Jas 4:6–8 and 1 Pet 5:5–9).[39]

As these references indicate, scholars identify somewhat different passages as examples of early Christian ritual or catechesis, and they interpret them differently. The references suggest, however, that James may well have been in close touch with the life of the early church.

This survey of sources and affinities suggests that the author of James was in contact with the popular Hellenistic culture of the day. It suggests further that he was influenced by a rich religious heritage from the Old Testament and Judaism. Many recent interpreters stress that James was interested in the ethical aspects of Jewish law rather than its ritual and ceremonial aspects. Similarly, recent interpreters are more inclined to identify parallels between the ethical admonitions in James and the teachings of Jesus at a preliterary stage in the formation of synoptic tradition.

Topics for continuing investigation include the influence of the wisdom tradition on James and reflections of early Christian ritual and catechesis.

Occasion and Setting

During the period covered by this book, scholars have offered different explanations of the religious identity and geographical location of the early Christians to whom James was sent. The address "to the twelve tribes in the dispersion" (1:1) seems to suggest that the letter was intended for Jewish Christians scattered or "dispersed" outside Palestine. A number of interpreters, although by no means all, understand the address in this sense.

Peter H. Davids believes James fits into a Palestinian setting during the last three decades before the first Jewish War. He envisages a situation in which the early Christians are suffering trials, including persecution of the poor by the rich. He seems to locate the letter in Palestine itself, as the city is torn by party strife involving pro-Roman high-priestly families and anti-Roman Zealots. In this situation, Davids believes, James writes to encourage his readers to turn from the world and nurture unity and love within the church.[40]

A number of other interpreters believe James addresses Jewish Christian communities outside Palestine. **Franz Mussner** suggests that James, writing from Jerusalem, is probably addressing Jewish Christian communities in Syria and the areas immediately north and northwest.[41] **Douglas J. Moo** sees the situation in the same general terms as Davids and Mussner, proposing that James of Jerusalem is writing to Jewish Christians who have left Palestine as a result of persecution (cf. Acts 11:19).[42]

Other interpreters modify the assumption that James addresses Jewish Christians. **Cain Hope Felder,** for example, believes that in the late 80s or 90s a redactor edited a sermon originally given by James of Jerusalem and distributed it as an encyclical. The redactor apparently sent this letter to churches of the Diaspora that were divided internally as Jewish and Gentile Christians sought to establish separate identities. The redactor, a devotee of James, sought to "alleviate tensions" for Jewish Christians and "mollify Gentile Christians" by downplaying cultic aspects of the law.[43]

Sophie Laws moves even further away from the assumption that James is a document of Jewish Christianity. As it was noted above, she believes that the background of the writer and his readers probably lies among the "God-fearers," non-Jews who were attracted to Judaism without becoming proselytes. Whenever these God-fearers converted to Christianity, they brought their knowledge of Judaism into their new faith. The letter of James, Laws believes, is addressed to people in this situation.[44]

At the opposite extreme from the idea of a Jewish Christian audience, **Burton Scott Easton** believes that James is probably addressed to Gentile Christians outside Palestine. He argues that the "elders of the church" (5:14) play a role in public worship that elders did not have in Jewish synagogues. In Judaism, elders interpreted and administered the law, but they did not officiate in public worship.

Easton notes that in James the elders pray for a sick person and anoint the person with oil (5:14). They have, in effect,

assumed a function in public worship. This non-Jewish development could occur only in Christianity, and probably only in Gentile Christian communities outside Palestine.[45] Subsequent
interpreters of James do not seem to have addressed Easton's
argument.

A number of commentators understand "the twelve tribes in
the dispersion" (1:1) in a figurative sense to designate all Christians
as the spiritual Israel or the eschatological people of God. **Franz
Mussner** notes that it was part of Jewish eschatological hope that
the Messiah would restore Israel as the twelve-tribe league. James
sees this hope fulfilled in the Christian community. "For him,"
Mussner writes, "it is the twelve-tribe people, the eschatological
Israel in the messianic time of salvation."[46] Perkins, Barnett, and
Cantinat give similar interpretations of the letter's address.[47]

Just as interpreters differ in identifying the recipients of the
letter, they also differ in reconstructing their circumstances. James
speaks, for example, of "the early and the late rain" (5:7 [RSV]),
referring to periods of rainfall in October–November and
April–May. Leahy and Davids understand this as an indication that
the writer was familiar with agricultural conditions in Palestine
and southern Syria. Laws, however, sees it as a general biblical
allusion.[48]

Scholars also differ in explaining the trials or oppression to
which the recipients are subjected. Easton, Davids, and Johnson
believe that the recipients are economically poor and are being
oppressed by the wealthy. More specifically, Davids suggests that
Christians are being persecuted by wealthy Jews in Palestine during the period before 70 CE. Reicke seems to be alone among
modern scholars in correlating the trials or persecutions in James
with political conditions prevailing toward the close of the reign
of Domitian.[49]

Sophie Laws has made an ambitious attempt to describe the
sociological situation of the author and readers of James. She
locates their setting in "the multicultural environment of the Hellenistic cities," discounting the references to agriculture (5:4, 7)

as metaphorical allusions. The letter envisages an established community that holds meetings (2:2), recognizes "teachers" (3:1), and has "elders" (5:14) as leaders. The members would doubtless consider themselves among "the poor," but they are ready to welcome the rich to their meetings. Perhaps they are too willing to do so, as the author's attack on the rich (2:6–7; 5:1–3) may indicate.

The members, Laws continues, are not being persecuted for their faith. They experience oppression and abuse as a reflection of legal and economic pressures imposed by the powerful on the disadvantaged. The assumption that their meetings are open to visitors indicates that they have not been forced into a ghetto. Tensions arise not from doctrinal disputes but from personal relationships in a small society—anger (1:19–20), jealousy (4:1–2), and slander and criticism (4:11–12).[50]

Whether or not one agrees with all the details of this reconstruction, Laws clearly illustrates how a scholar with sensitivity to the perspectives of the social sciences can delineate significant aspects of an early Christian community.

Genre and Structure

During the period covered by this book, scholars have shown an increasing interest in redefining the genre of James and identifying broader patterns of structure in the letter as a whole. Earlier commentators tended to see James as a series of ethical admonitions, sometimes organized into loose collections. Later commentators tend to find the origins of the letter in some form of continuous oral communication, such as the sermon or discourse, and they are more inclined to find broader patterns of organization throughout the letter.

Martin Dibelius, who published the first edition of his commentary in 1921, understands James primarily as an example of paraenesis—that is, "a text which strings together admonitions of general ethical content." Characteristics of this genre include a pervasive eclecticism (selections from the ethical tradition), lack of continuity of thought, formal connections such as catchwords, and the absence of a single audience and a single set of circumstances. Dibelius finds no continuity of thought in the letter as a whole, although he does speak of three "treatises" (2:1—3:12), which he regards as expansions of paraenetic sayings presented in diatribe form.[51]

In a similar vein, **Burton Scott Easton** regards James as a perfect example of paraenesis, occasionally combined with the diatribe. He sees the letter as a collection of sayings, sayings groups, or brief treatments of topics such as reverence for the poor (2:1–12), the relation of faith and works (2:14–26), and sins of the tongue (3:1–2). Easton finds, however, no logical plan to explain the sequence of ideas. Indeed, he can identify no "general theme" in the letter.[52]

Other commentators, such as **Franz Mussner** and **Jean Cantinat,** also understand James primarily as a collection of paraenetic materials. Mussner does seek to find some unifying principle in the letter. The idea that ties together the individual examples of paraenesis is "a living Christianity of deed." In his emphasis on this principle, the author stands in a "rich tradition" that he received from the "living piety of Judaism."[53]

Along the same lines as Mussner, **Albert E. Barnett** proposes that the theme of James is "the righteousness of God," in the sense of the human righteousness that God approves. Piety, he believes, should be "effective" rather than exclusively intellectual or devotional. This piety is a synthesis of endurance (1:2–18), obedience (1:19–27), impartiality (2:1–13), integrity (2:14–26), discipline (3:1—4:10), humility (4:11—5:6), patience (5:7–11), prayerfulness (5:12–18), and love (5:19–20).

In giving this list of components of "effective piety," Barnett also provides an outline of the letter. He divides it into sections, listing nine virtues of Christian life. His analysis represents a decisive move away from the form-critical judgment that James lacks a sequence of ideas or a general theme.[54]

In a similar way, **Leo G. Perdue** seeks to go beyond the idea that paraenesis conveys admonitions that are traditional in nature and generalized in application. He wishes instead to delineate the social settings in which paraenesis functions. "The paraenesis of James," he writes, "exhorts the audience to reflect upon their initial entrance into the community, to continue to dissociate themselves from the world, and to engage in more committed efforts to strive towards a higher level of virtue and perfection." Perdue develops this insight by suggesting that the primary function of paraenesis is socialization, which occurs when a person joins new social groups and internalizes their norms and values. Socialization provides moral direction, defines the identity of the new social group, and legitimizes the new social world that the group represents. Perdue gives several examples of socialization in James. Chapter 4 provides moral direction for new members. The attack on wealthy landowners (5:1ff.) uses the strategy of in-group, out-group conflict to define group boundaries and strengthen cohesion. The references to Abraham and Rahab (2:21ff.) as famous Jewish examples of virtue serve to legitimize the new social world into which the novices are being initiated.[55]

Some recent interpreters also believe that the "letter" of James originated in some form of oral communication. **Thomas W. Leahy,** for example, sees it as an example of "early Judaeo-Christian exhortatory preaching," emphasizing the practical consequences of Christian faith. Leahy is inclined to think of James the brother of Jesus as the source of this material.[56]

Peter H. Davids thinks of the letter as a two–stage work, in which James the brother of Jesus could have taken some of his own homilies, sayings, and maxims and compiled them into the form of an epistle. Through this theory Davids seeks to account for the diversity of materials that Dibelius found and then identify some redactional unity in the letter as a whole. He views the final product as a literary epistle—that is, a tract intended for publication—rather than an actual letter.[57]

In a similar way, **Cain Hope Felder** believes that the basis of the letter was a sermon by James the brother of Jesus in the months before his martyrdom in Jerusalem. Then in the late 80s or 90s a redactor, skilled in Hellenistic Greek, edited this sermon in the style of an encyclical. Felder does not outline the letter but does identify major themes, such as holistic Christianity (involving faith and deeds), personal speech-ethics, social righteousness, and distinctions between rich and poor.[58]

Luke Timothy Johnson also finds the basis of James in a type of oral communication, arguing that it is best understood "as a form of protreptic discourse in the form of a letter." This kind of discourse, he explains, seeks to persuade members of an audience to live up to the profession of faith that they have made. Since Johnson considers it very likely that James the brother of Jesus was the author of the letter, he would envisage James as addressing an audience of new Christians and urging them to remain faithful to their commitments.

Although Johnson does not outline the letter, he believes the first chapter is programmatic because it introduces a number of topics that are developed more fully in following chapters. These include the themes of prayer (1:5–7; 5:13–18), rich and poor (1:9–10; 2:1–6; 4:13 – 5:6), the tongue (1:19–20; 3:1–12), and faith and deeds (1:22–27; 2:14–26). The final statement (5:19–20) serves as an appropriate conclusion.[59]

Douglas J. Moo evidently agrees with Davids and Johnson that James originated as a sermon or homily. He believes the central theme of the letter is "spiritual wholeness"—that is, James' concern that his readers not compromise with worldly values but dedicate themselves completely to God. This theme, Moo believes, runs throughout the letter and gives it a sense of unity.[60]

Recent interpreters of James have sought to move beyond a form-critical approach that divides the letter into discrete units of paraenesis and diatribe. With or without theories of two-stage development, they have looked for some type of redactional unity in the letter. A number of interpreters believe the letter originated in oral communication, and a number have also sought to analyze its structure. Although the analyses differ from one another, they do reflect a concern to identify a sequence of ideas and general themes in the letter of James.

Faith and Works

A survey of this kind should include modern assessments of the criticism that Martin Luther made of the letter of James. Luther found a direct contradiction between James 2:24 (a person is "justified by works and not by faith alone") and Galatians 2:16 (a person is "not justified by works of law but through faith in Christ Jesus" [author's translation]). Believing that James rejected Paul's doctrine of justification by faith, Luther attacked the letter as "an epistle of straw" in his Preface to the New Testament of 1522. He placed it at the end of his translation of the New Testament, along with Hebrews, Jude, and Revelation, which he equally disliked.[61]

During the period covered by this book, there do not seem to have been any commentators who support Luther's idea of a direct contradiction between Paul and James. Modern scholars are more likely to argue that Paul and James were addressing different situations and were using terms differently. They also find an essential similarity, if not a complete identity, in the perceptions of Christian faith and life that each articulated.

Reconstructing the situations that Paul and James are addressing, **George Eldon Ladd** states that "James and Paul are dealing with two different situations: Paul with the self-righteousness of Jewish legal piety and James with dead orthodoxy."[62] In a similar vein, **Peter H. Davids** argues that Paul and James are discussing totally different subjects. Paul is addressing the reception of Gentiles into the church without circumcision, whereas James treats the problem of failure of works of charity within the church.[63]

In a broader sense, some interpreters emphasize that James is less concerned to oppose faith and works than to contrast two types of faith. "James," remarks **Thomas W. Leahy,** "is not opposing faith and works, but living faith and dead faith."[64] Similarly, **R. A. Martin** writes that James is contrasting a faith that issues in works and a faith that claims to exist independently of works.[65] Although Paul and James both speak in terms of faith and works, these commentators emphasize the importance of identifying the polarities that each has in mind.

Some recent interpreters also argue that Paul and James use terms differently. **Burton Scott Easton** believes, for example, that Paul thinks of faith as a person's self-surrender to God, and he views justification as the initial part of spiritual life, involving acceptance by God. James, in contrast, regards faith as an intellectual acceptance of monotheism, and justification as the progression or end of spiritual life.[66]

In a similar vein, **George Eldon Ladd** writes that for Paul works are "Jewish deeds of formal obedience to the Law that provide man a basis for boasting in his good achievements." For James, in contrast, works are "deeds that fulfill the 'royal law' of love for the neighbor."[67]

Although Paul and James address different situations and use terms differently, interpreters tend to look for the basic understanding of Christianity that they both share. Many believe that Paul and James agree in regarding faith, made possible by God's grace, as the basis of Christian life. Paul speaks of the priority of grace or faith in a number of key passages—for example, Romans 3:21–25; Galatians 2:16. The question is whether James also thinks of grace or faith as the starting-point and continuing context of Christian life.

Adolf Schlatter calls attention to several passages in James presenting faith itself as a gift from God. A person, for example, prays for wisdom (1:5), and God grants the gift of the wisdom that comes from above and enables one to do good works (3:17). A person is born anew through God's will (1:18), and through God's election the person becomes a believer (2:5). Passages such as these emphasize God's initiative in making possible the new life of faith.[68]

In a similar way, **Peter H. Davids** writes that James "never argues that the essence of Christianity is anything other than a commitment to God in Christ or a reception of grace from God." Davids calls special attention to the themes of regeneration through God's action in his Word (1:18), salvation through the "implanted word" (1:21), and God's gift of grace to the repentant (4:6). None of these ideas, he emphasizes, is at variance from Paul.[69]

Franz Mussner also focuses on the "implanted word that has the power to save your souls" (1:21). The main purpose of the letter, he believes, is to promote the "realization" of this word as Christians seek to give expression to their faith in everyday life.[70] Here Mussner—who as much as anyone emphasizes the inseparability of faith and works in James—clearly thinks in terms of the priority of God's gift of his "implanted word" as the basis of Christian life.

If Paul and James agree that God's grace or faith is the starting-point for Christian life, they would also agree that faith must express itself in "works" or good deeds. Paul not only emphasizes the importance of "faith working through love" (Gal 5:6), but he also states that God is "at work" in the Christian believer, both "to will" and "to work" for his gracious purposes (Phil 2:13). The idea of expressing faith in deeds of loving service is so important for Paul that he thinks of God himself as motivating and facilitating this process in the Christian believer.

The author of James also emphasizes that faith must express itself in deeds of service, such as loving one's neighbor or obeying the commandments of the Decalogue (2:8–13). If it does not do this, faith is "dead" (2:17) or "barren" (2:20). "True faith," Davids observes, "reveals itself in pious deeds of love, as the examples of Abraham and Rahab show."[71] Conversely, as **R. A. Martin** notes, "works are not a substitute for faith, but are the evidence of faith."[72]

Whereas modern interpreters emphasize that Paul and James both think in terms of a close relation between faith and works, **Dan O. Via Jr.** believes that they hold different views of human nature. These differences, in turn, affect their perceptions of faith and justification.

Via argues that Paul, in his understanding of faith as a "total unified response" to the gospel, perceives that a person's well-being resides in wholeness. James, in calling for faith and works as two kinds of cooperating responses, "fails to see the need for wholeness." Via holds that James "lacks an understanding of faith and of the wholeness of man which would prevent works of love from becoming a condition for justification."[73]

Via does not, of course, deny the importance of faith for James. His emphasis on the "wholeness" of human nature and the need for a holistic response to the gospel strikes a cautionary note against a tendency simply to identify the perspectives of Paul and James.

Major Characteristics and Concerns

This survey of scholarship on James concludes by calling attention to several studies that highlight the continuing significance of James by placing it more broadly in its environment or correlating it with recent movements in religious thought.

Luke Timothy Johnson helps readers appreciate the distinctiveness of James by describing four ways in which it stands out in ancient moral literature. He notes that James is concerned, first, with morality itself, rather than with "manners" as a key to success and honor. Second, it addresses the church, an intentional community defined by shared values and convictions, rather than the household or the state. Third, James is egalitarian rather than hierarchical, limiting kinship language to "brother" and "sister." Finally, James is communitarian rather than individualistic, emphasizing solidarity and compassion rather than self-assertion.[74] Johnson's comments are especially helpful in providing a broader perspective on a letter that often presents so many critical and exegetical difficulties.

In an afterword to the fifth edition of his commentary, dated 1987, **Franz Mussner** relates James to the dialogic movement in modern philosophy that is concerned with the "I–Thou" relation. Referring especially to the Jewish philosopher Emmanuel Levinas, Mussner notes that in this type of thought the "Other," the "Thou," moves into the field of view and becomes present, not as an "it" that stands at one's disposal but as an individual person, a "face" or "countenance" that meets one and calls one to respond.

Relating this philosophical movement to the letter of James, Mussner says that "a basic interest of the letter of James is precisely the Other, the concern for the one who exists in physical or spiritual need…Community for James is community of brothers, in which one is there for the other, the neighbor." Mussner develops this perspective by referring to James' concern for the poor, the centrality of the commandment to love one's neighbor, and an understanding of justification based on faith and works of love.[75]

Identifying another major theme in James, **William R. Baker** devotes a full-length study to "personal speech-ethics" or simply "speech-ethics." He uses these expressions "to capture the idea of ethics or morality as applied to interpersonal communication." This approach analyzes the relationship of speech to thoughts and actions. It also reflects the predominance of the spoken word as the primary means of communication in the ancient Mediterranean world.

Baker argues that James has special concerns for controlling speech, listening to the "implanted word" of God, translating the words of God or Jesus into deeds, avoiding the negative aspects of the power of words, and recognizing their positive aspects. He suggests further that a distinctive emphasis in James is the close relation between speech-ethics and a person's spiritual and ethical development.[76]

In an interesting attempt to apply a paradigm from Old Testament study to the interpretation of James, **Douglas J. Moo** calls attention to the theme of "covenantal nomism" that **E. P. Sanders** described in 1977. Sanders used this expression to indicate that the people of Israel were to obey the law *(nomos)* in grateful response to God's grace. They did so not to gain entrance to the covenant, but to remain within the covenant that God had freely given.[77]

Moo argues that this paradigm is generally accurate but applies only to the covenant and not to ultimate salvation, which depends on God's decision at the time of judgment. To receive this salvation, Jews had to follow the law. Judaism, in the period following the rebuilding of the Jerusalem temple in 520–515 BCE, was synergistic — "it required was synergistic — "it required human beings to cooperate with God's grace through obedience to the law for salvation."

Moo believes that James gives a Christian understanding of this synergistic form of covenantal nomism. The Christian life has its basis in God's grace (1:18) and faith in Christ (2:1), but Christians must obey the "royal law" (2:8) to receive salvation at the judgment of God.

Rather unexpectedly, Moo goes on to argue that the synergism of James is only apparent. What James says can be read in light of the "monergism" of Paul (i.e., the principle that God himself provides salvation). James' teaching on works can be seen in relation to Paul's belief that works are the product of God's grace through the indwelling Holy Spirit (e.g., Phil 2:13). For this reason, Moo concludes, Paul and James are complementary.[78]

These observations by Johnson, Mussner, Baker, and Moo invite critical reflection and perhaps further study. Whether or not one agrees with the observations in detail, they illustrate how modern scholars can place the insights of James in broader perspective and correlate them with other areas of religious study.

2
1 Peter

Recent scholarship on 1 Peter may be treated under the headings of authorship and date, occasion and setting, the question of a liturgical basis, the role of Christians in society, the meaning of "the spirits in prison" (3:19) and "the dead" (4:6), and major characteristics and concerns. As in the case of the letter of James, it is sometimes possible to identify areas of agreement or trends in interpretation. In other instances it is possible only to describe the different views that scholars have proposed.

Authorship and Date

The "traditional" view of authorship is that the apostle Peter (1:1), with help from Silvanus (5:12), wrote the letter in Rome sometime between the martyrdom of Paul about 62 CE and the outbreak of persecution under Nero in 64 CE.

For the sake of analysis, **Archibald M. Hunter** summarizes four objections to this view: 1) the letter shows a knowledge of the Greek language that Peter would not have; 2) it is indebted to Paul's theology; 3) it does not bear the marks of one who knew Jesus and heard his teaching; 4) it implies a time when the mere profession of Christianity was a crime — that is, the first decade of the second century.[1]

Hunter responds as follows to these objections: 1) Although Peter himself may have a limited knowledge of Greek, he says explicitly that he is writing the letter "by Silvanus" (5:12 [RSV]). There is no reason to doubt that Silvanus is the person named, with Paul and Timothy, as a joint author of 1 and 2 Thessalonians. Known as "Silas" in Acts, he is a prominent member of the church in Jerusalem and a helper of Paul on his second missionary journey. Silvanus is clearly able to write the literary Greek of the letter.

2) The "Paulinism" of 1 Peter is really "common, apostolic Christianity." The epistle 1 Peter does not show clear dependence on Romans and Ephesians, as some scholars claim. Further, some Pauline doctrines, such as justification by faith, are absent from 1 Peter. If there are echoes of Paul in 1 Peter, these reflect Silvanus' long association with Paul.

Further, 3) 1 Peter contains many references to the life and teachings of Jesus. The writer probably shows a knowledge of the trial of Jesus (2:21–24), the Transfiguration (5:1), the command of the risen Lord in John 21:17 (5:2), and the foot-washing (5:5). The letter also has at least ten echoes of Jesus' sayings.

4) The references to suffering and persecution in 1 Peter are quite general, and they need not reflect more than malevolence and abuse by the public. Even if they involve persecution by the state, they could refer to conditions under Nero.[2]

For these reasons Hunter affirms the traditional view of authorship. "The general tone and temper of the epistle," he writes, "suggests that it comes down to us from the early days of the faith, nor can any of the objections raised against Petrine authorship be sustained." He believes that Peter wrote the letter in Rome, between the death of Paul in 62 CE and the beginning of the Neronian persecution in 64 CE. The fact that Peter counsels loyalty to the emperor (2:13–17) indicates that he was writing before the outbreak of this persecution.[3]

Hunter's support of the traditional theory is typical of the views of many scholars. Sometimes interpreters employ the same general arguments as Hunter, but they give a slightly different emphasis to some detail or call attention to an additional point. Collectively, they provide further support for the traditional view.

Edward G. Selwyn, for example, assigns a more substantive role to Silvanus in the composition of the letter. The "governing mind and character" of the letter, he believes, are those of the apostle Peter, but the "matter as well as its style" reveal the influence of Silvanus. Like Hunter, Selwyn dates the letter between 62 and 64 CE.[4]

W. C. van Unnik calls attention to the theory that 1 Peter is addressed to Christians who were "God-fearers," with connections to Jewish synagogues. This theory, he believes, fits in with the description of Peter as specially commissioned for the Christian mission among the Jews (Gal 2:7). It supports the view that Peter wrote the letter, probably about 60 CE.[5]

Bo Reicke and **Joseph A. Fitzmyer** note that the role of Silvanus would explain the use of the Septuagint for Old Testament quotations. In this way they can argue for authorship by the apostle Peter, while acknowledging that Peter himself would probably not quote from the Septuagint.[6]

Norman Hillyer notes that the early church emphasized apostolic authorship as a criterion for canonical status. It is significant, he believes, that it accepted 1 Peter but rejected other writings attributed to Peter, such as the *Gospel of Peter,* the *Acts of Peter,* and the *Apocalypse of Peter.* Although Hillyer believes that complete certainty is unattainable, he thinks that the "burden of demonstration" lies with those who regard the letter as pseudonymous.[7]

In contrast to the advocates for traditional views, other scholars argue that a later, anonymous author wrote the letter in the name of the apostle Peter. **Leonhard Goppelt,** for example, would date 1 Peter between 65 and 80 CE. He bases his argument especially on the mixture of church offices in the letter, in which charismatic forms of service (4:10–11) are combined with a form of organization involving elders (5:1–5).[8]

More recently, **David L. Bartlett** lists several reasons pointing to a later author: the sophisticated Greek style, the use of the

Septuagint, and the absence of Jewish/Gentile controversies so prominent in Paul's time. Bartlett also emphasizes that the recipients seem to be suffering from local harassment rather than governmental persecution. He concludes that 1 Peter is probably later than Paul but earlier than Revelation and Pliny's correspondence with Trajan—that is, possibly about 90 CE.[9]

As a variant of the theory of anonymous authorship, some interpreters suggest that a Petrine group or "school" produced the letter in Rome. **John H. Elliott** believes that this group included Silvanus, Mark, and an unnamed "sister" (5:12–13). This group sent the letter in the name of Peter, possibly between 73 and 92 CE.[10]

Elliott gives three main reasons for his view. He notes first that the large size of the area mentioned in 1:1 suggests a substantial growth in missionary work beyond the limits reached by Paul. This suggests in turn that 1 Peter was written decades after Paul's time. Elliott also argues that the use of "Babylon" for "Rome" in 5:13 indicates a later date, since this use of "Babylon" occurs only in writings composed after the fall of Jerusalem in 70 CE (i.e., the *Sibylline Oracles,* 2 Baruch, 4 Ezra, and Revelation).

Elliott argues, thirdly, that the type of expression used in 5:12 ("through, by *[dia]* Silvanus") conventionally identifies the emissary who delivers a letter. There would be no reason, therefore, to regard Silvanus as Peter's secretary and possibly co-author. Elliott does believe that Silvanus and Mark were probably the same persons associated with Peter in Jerusalem and now reunited with him in Rome. The mention of these persons, together with the unnamed "sister," indicates that 1 Peter is the product of a group or circle that once gathered about the apostle Peter and now transmits his witness.[11]

Paul J. Achtemeier believes that the best working hypothesis is anonymous authorship of 1 Peter, perhaps by one or more members of a Petrine school in Rome. This school, he suggests, produced a pseudonymous letter drawing on traditions historically associated with Simon Peter.

If the letter is pseudonymous, Achtemeier continues, it may have been written between 80 and 100 CE. Lack of clear reference to martyrdom could place it before Pliny's persecution of Christians in Bithynia around 112–114. Pliny's reference, about 110, to the defection of some Christians twenty five years earlier would also point to this period.[12]

Disagreements among specialists indicate that the question of authorship and date remains a topic for continuing investigation. It is interesting that 1 Peter raises some of the same issues as James—for example, whether someone from Galilee could write literary Greek of a high quality. In 1 Peter, the mention of Silvanus may provide an answer to this question, if indeed Silvanus had the role of scribe.

Occasion and Setting

Issues involved in describing the occasion and setting of 1 Peter include the religious and cultural background of the recipients, their political, legal, and social status, and the type of harassment or persecution to which they are subjected.

Archibald M. Hunter notes that 1 Peter is addressed to Christians in five districts of Asia Minor—Pontus, Galatia, Cappadocia, Asia, and Bithynia (1:1). Most of the addressees, he believes, are of Gentile background. The letter seeks to encourage them to be steadfast when persecution breaks out. In a similar vein, **Joseph A. Fitzmyer** and **Pheme Perkins** also identify the recipients as Christians of Gentile background. Like Hunter, they emphasize that the addresses are facing a situation of persecution.[13]

W. C. van Unnik agrees that the recipients have a general background in the Gentile world. More specifically, he considers it possible that they are "God-fearers"—that is, Gentiles who are attracted to Judaism but do not become proselytes. Van Unnik believes that 1:18–19 probably refers to a sacrifice connected with proselyte conversion. This sacrifice, he holds, went out of use after 70 CE, and the reference here must indicate that 1 Peter was written before that time.[14]

In a variation of this view, **Scot McKnight** holds that most of the recipients are Gentile God-fearers but others are former Jews. Without referring to God-fearers, **Edward G. Selwyn** and **John H. Elliott** suggest that some recipients are Christians of Gentile background and others are Christians of Jewish background.[15]

Some interpreters of 1 Peter have employed a method of sociological exegesis that focuses on the interaction between the early Christian movement and its social environment. Elliott explains that this approach "seeks to discover the manner in which a given document has been designed as a response to a given situation, and how it has been composed to elicit a social response on the part of its audience."

From this perspective Elliott focuses on the political, legal, and social status of the recipients of 1 Peter. He notes that they are described in 2:11 as "resident aliens" *(paroikoi)* and "visiting strangers" *(parepidemoi)*. As such, they are second-class or marginalized persons, with limited rights and social standing. Elliott emphasizes that they held this status before their conversion, and now they receive encouragement from their new faith to continue as an oppressed minority in society.[16]

In contrast to Elliott, **Paul J. Achtemeier** questions whether the terms "resident aliens" and "visiting strangers" refer in the first instance to the preconversion political and social status of the recipients of 1 Peter. Pointing to the word "as" in 2:11 ("as aliens and strangers"), he argues that these expressions should be understood as a metaphorical reflection of the faith and history of Israel.

Achtemeier's argument reflects his conviction that "Israel" is the controlling metaphor in the theology of 1 Peter. He thinks here of "Israel" as a totality, not simply as a forerunner of the Christian community or an independent entity. "In 1 Peter," he writes, "the language and hence the reality of Israel pass without remainder into the language and hence the reality of the new people of God." Achtemeier believes that the writer of 1 Peter chose the terms "resident aliens" and "visiting strangers" because they refer to "Israel" as the controlling metaphor for the Christian community.[17]

In his 1957 commentary, **Archibald M. Hunter** interpreted "aliens and strangers" to mean that Christians do not really belong in this world but will have their true home in heaven.[18] Recent scholars occasionally mention this older view, but they usually prefer to understand these terms as referring in some way to the situation of Christians in the present.

Most recent scholars believe that the recipients of 1 Peter were facing persecution in the form of localized suspicion, slander, or harassment from non-Christian neighbors. They reject the view that the recipients were subjected to official persecution by state authorities, whether under Nero (64 CE), Domitian (95 CE), or Pliny in Bithynia (ca. 110 CE).

W. C. van Unnik offers several cogent arguments in favor of unofficial harassment and abuse. He notes that 1 Peter regards the whole church throughout the world as sharing in the same sufferings (5:9). Van Unnik argues that all state persecutions before the third century were more or less local. The sufferings mentioned in 1 Peter, therefore, must have had another character.

Van Unnik also argues that the advice to obey the government (2:13–17) implies "a very positive relation with the state authorities." The advice assumes that political authorities will acknowledge the good conduct of Christians and commend them as good citizens.

As a third argument, van Unnik maintains that the sufferings mentioned in 1 Peter "all belong to the personal sphere; they are the results of evil feelings and hatred against people who do not follow the general line…" Van Unnik concludes, "No state persecution in any period is reflected in the letter."[19]

With minor variations, recent scholars agree in understanding persecution in 1 Peter in terms of local suspicion and harassment rather than official governmental policy under Nero,

Domitian, or Pliny. This is the case with **C. F. D. Moule, Edward G. Selwyn, Joseph A. Fitzmyer, Claude H. Thompson, George Eldon Ladd, John H. Elliott, Pheme Perkins,** and **Paul J. Achtemeier.** Thompson and Ladd mention the possibility that some official persecution may be involved, as well as unofficial abuse. Selwyn and Achtemeier think in terms of unofficial harassment from the general populace with occasional intervention by local officials.[20]

The Question of a Liturgical Basis

During the early part of the period covered by this study, a number of interpreters supported the theory that 1 Peter had its origin, at least in part, in an early Christian baptismal address or liturgy. This theory evidently goes back to **Richard Perdelwitz,** who argued in 1911 that 1 Peter 1:3—4:11 reflects an address given to candidates at a baptismal ceremony. Perdelwitz called attention to the mention of baptism in 3:21, and also pointed to expressions that he interpreted as references to baptism ("born anew," 1:3, 23 [RSV]; "newborn babes," 2:2 [RSV]). He also noted temporal expressions that seemed to suggest the recent reception of baptism ("now," 1:12; 2:10, 25; 3:21 [RSV]; "at the present time," 1:6, 8 [author's translation]).[21]

A few years later **Wilhelm Bornemann,** apparently without any knowledge of the study by Perdelwitz, argued in 1919 that 1 Peter 1:3—5:11 was originally a baptismal address, based on Psalm 34, delivered by Silvanus about 90 CE in a city of Asia Minor. Using many of the same arguments as Perdelwitz, Bornemann differed primarily in the belief that almost the entire letter represented a baptismal sermon.[22]

Hans Windisch combined the theory of a baptismal address with a special emphasis on paraenesis. He regarded the major part of the letter, 1:3—4:11, as a baptismal address incorporating two types of paraenesis. A group of four passages (1:13–21; 1:22–25; 2:1–10; 4:1–6) represented paraenesis directed to the candidates for baptism, urging them to follow a holy way of life in light of their new Christian faith. The address also incorporated elements of paraenesis directed to the entire congregation (2:13—3:7; 4:7–11).[23]

Herbert Preisker, the editor of the third edition (1951) of Windisch's commentary, added a supplement in which he developed Windisch's analysis of 1:3—4:11 as a baptismal address. Preisker argued that 1:3—4:11 was the account of an early Christian worship service for the baptized, with the actual ceremony of baptism occurring after 1:21. This service was followed by a service for the entire congregation (4:12—5:11).[24]

Several years later, in 1954, **Frank L. Cross** went a step further, with his theory that 1 Peter 1:3—4:11 gives the celebrant's part of a paschal, or Easter, liturgy that included the rite of baptism and the celebration of the Eucharist. This service was evidently an Easter Vigil, beginning in the darkness of Holy Saturday and ending on Easter morning. Cross emphasizes that in the early church the paschal liturgy was a regular occasion for baptism.

On the basis of his theory, Cross gives the following outline of 1 Peter 1:3—4:11: the celebrant's (bishop's) opening prayer (1:3–12); his charge to the candidates (1:13–21, with the actual baptism occurring after 1:21); his welcome to the newly baptized (1:22–25); his discourse on the sacramental life (2:1–10, with the Communion of the newly baptized occurring after 2:10); and his address to the newly baptized on the duties of Christian discipleship (2:11—4:11). Although he is not certain, Cross suggests that the second section of the letter, beginning at 4:12, may be an address to the entire congregation.[25]

A few other writers support the view of 1 Peter as a baptismal liturgy in general or an Easter festival in particular. **M.E. Boismard** finds citations or reflections of a baptismal hymn (1:3–5) and a baptismal catechism (1:13—2:10). **Edward G. Selwyn** finds a cultic reference to the "celebration of the Pascha or Feast of Redemption, of which baptism was a part." He notes also that the Eucharist was perhaps included, as 2:3–5 suggests. Similarly,

Claude H. Thompson finds some "liturgical purpose" in the letter, especially with regard to baptism and Holy Communion.[26]

Frank L. Cross may be regarded as the major representative of the baptismal-Eucharistic-paschal interpretation of 1 Peter. Although he had some supporters, a number of other scholars have severely criticized his thesis. Prominent among these are **C. F. D. Moule** and **T. C. G. Thornton.**

Moule agrees that 1 Peter includes baptism in its general understanding of Christian life. He argues, however, that this does not have to involve an actual baptismal or baptismal-Eucharistic liturgy. He maintains that it is difficult to understand how a liturgy or homily, without its rubrics, could have been "hastily dressed up as a letter" and sent off to Christians who did not know its original setting.

Moule also argues that the reference to suffering in 4:16 does not require the paschal motif to explain it. Words meaning "now" do not necessarily mean that a baptismal rite is in progress; they can simply contrast the past with the present. Similarly, the expression "newborn babes" can be merely a general reference to baptized Christians.[27]

Thornton questions whether 1 Peter is in any sense paschal. He maintains that the reference to Christ as "lamb" in 1:18–19 is not necessarily a reference to the Passover lamb, noting that lambs were used at other sacrifices besides Passover, and a lamb was not the only possible Passover sacrifice. Thornton argues also that references to baptism do not necessarily have paschal overtones, since evidence that Easter was an especially appropriate time for baptism appears no earlier than Tertullian.

In a more general sense, Thornton questions whether 1 Peter represents a baptismal liturgy. He believes that "…the mere fact that 1 Peter uses baptismal language does not make it part of a first-century church service." The writer, he argues, uses baptismal imagery because his main concern is to provide ethical instruction, and baptismal language and ethical language often went together in the early church.[28]

Other interpreters also tend to question the theory of a baptismal or baptismal-Eucharistic-paschal liturgy. **Thomas W. Leahy** thinks of 1 Peter as probably a straightforward literary composition (1:3—4:11), followed by a separate section of encouragement for those under persecution. **John H. Elliott** and **R. A. Martin** point out that no other contemporary examples of a baptismal homily or liturgy are available. Similarly, **William J. Dalton** questions whether a "baptismal liturgy-homily" existed as a "literary genre" at the end of the first century, much less in apostolic times.[29]

The possibility that 1 Peter reflects an actual worship service—a baptismal homily or liturgy, or a baptismal-Eucharistic-paschal liturgy—may be seen as an intriguing theory that enjoyed some popularity around the beginning of the period covered by this book. Sharp criticisms of this thesis, together perhaps with emerging interests in other areas of interpretation, have led to a trend in recent decades to abandon the theory.

The Role of Christians in Society

An exciting recent development in the study of 1 Peter has been the attempt to define the role that the author believes Christians should play in relation to society. Because the writer speaks of the recipients as, in some sense, "resident aliens" and "visiting strangers," he must assume that they do not simply identify with the surrounding culture. Because he indicates that they are facing some form of persecution, he implies that they must decide how to relate to their non-Christian neighbors. In light of these conditions, recent scholarship has sought to delineate as precisely as possible how the writer of 1 Peter advises his readers to interact with their society.

In his 1957 commentary, **Archibald M. Hunter** suggests the words "aliens and strangers" (2:11) imply that Christians have their real home in heaven rather than here on earth. Noting that modern Christians are very much concerned with improvement of conditions in this world, Hunter advocates the principle of a "middle way" as a strategy for interacting with the cultural envi-ronment. In this way, Christians can find a balance between this-worldly and other-worldly perspectives.[30]

In his 1981 study of 1 Peter, **John H. Elliott** presents a view of the Christians' relation to society that may be described as "social nonconformity." Focusing on the description of the recip-ients as "resident aliens" and "visiting strangers" (2:11), Elliott argues that they receive limited political and legal rights and reduced social status. They also suffer slander and reproach from their non-Christian neighbors.[31]

The author of 1 Peter, Elliott believes, stresses the need for these early Christians to avoid social conformity and maintain their own distinctive identity as a community. They do not, how-ever, simply withdraw from the surrounding society. They are also to engage in positive, nonviolent interaction with their detractors in the hope of eventually winning them to the faith.[32]

The household code (2:13ff.) plays an important role in establishing the community's identity. It functions, Elliott sug-gests, to promote the internal solidarity of the Christian commu-nity, differentiate it more clearly from the standards and values of secular society, and relate the community to the broader ecclesio-logical concept of the "household" *(oikos)*.[33]

In these ways, Elliott believes, 1 Peter envisages a Christian community that will be "a home for the homeless, an *oikos* for the *paroikoi*." Such a "home" will provide a meaningful form of social identity, a basis of communal support, and an image of the Christian community in its entirety.[34]

In contrast to Elliott, **David L. Balch** develops an interpre-tation of 1 Peter that may be called "social conformity." Since the Romans tend to view Christianity as a new cult, Christians must conform to the expectations of society in order to escape criticism and persecution. For this reason, Balch argues, the author of 1 Peter writes to advise his readers "how they might become socially-politically acceptable to their society."[35]

Balch is especially concerned with the function of the household code (2:13ff.). The code addresses a situation in which certain slaves of pagan masters and wives of pagan husbands have converted to Christianity. Roman society reacted by accusing these persons of insubordination, perhaps sedition, and immorality. The code, Balch believes, seeks to inculcate an ethic that would render the behavior of slaves and wives acceptable to the standards of the surrounding society.[36]

Elliott and Balch published their interpretations of 1 Peter in 1981. At the meeting of the Society of Biblical Literature the following year, they engaged in a public discussion on the theme "1 Peter: Social Separation or Acculturation?" Their articles, published in 1986, give updated versions of their presentations at this meeting.

With regard to Balch's view that the household code in 1 Peter promotes Christian assimilation to secular values, Elliott argues that this attributes to the code an aim incompatible with the letter's general strategy. He maintains that his own view—that the code provides instruction for conduct and commitments typical of the Christian community—sees the code as part of a coherent argument developed throughout 1 Peter.

Elliott also questions Balch's assumption that the household code urges a "system linkage" between Christians and Roman society. He acknowledges that the code illustrates some points of such a "linkage." Elliott argues, however, that the code does not advocate such contacts as part of a program of social assimilation.[37]

For his part, Balch argues that Elliott focuses on dualistic contrasts, such as insiders and outsiders, the obedient and the disobedient, the righteous and sinners, and so on. Balch maintains that in "intercultural transmission," the receiving culture rejects some elements from the donor culture but accepts others. Thus 1 Peter rejects some aspects of pagan society (1:18; 4:3–4) but enthusiastically accepts others (2:12–14).

With reference to Elliott's view of the Christian community as "a home for the homeless," Balch states that the recipients of

1 Peter live in two "houses" or cultures. They live, to be sure, in the "spiritual house" of God. At the same time, they also live in a second, Graeco-Roman house, in which they seek to pursue peace and harmony as Christian slaves of pagan masters or Christian wives of pagan husbands.[38]

However one assesses the stimulating discussion between Elliott and Balch, it is interesting to note that some recent interpreters find value in both approaches. Their position might be labeled "identity and approval." **Pheme Perkins,** for example, believes that the new Christian community must be aware of how distinctive and special it is, yet the socioeconomic situation of its members makes it impossible to be isolated from society.[39] Similarly, **David L. Bartlett** writes that sectarian communities "do not necessarily choose between a strong sense of their unique identity and a desperate concern to be approved by the larger society."[40]

Whereas Elliott and Balch speak in terms of nonconformity and conformity, other interpreters analyze the relation to society in ways that do not quite coincide with these alternatives. **Leonhard Goppelt,** for instance, develops the idea of "responsible investment," as it might be called. Christians, he believes, live in society as foreigners. Yet they do not abandon society. As a witness of faith, they invest themselves responsibly within its institutions.[41]

In a similar way, **Paul J. Achtemeier** develops a position that could be described as "participation without compromise." As "aliens and strangers," Christians participate in society to the extent that they can do so without compromising their basic commitment to Christ as exclusive Lord. They do not seek to reform society but to show forth true goodness within it.[42]

David L. Bartlett believes that the terms "aliens and strangers" (2:11) express the relationship between Christians and the surrounding culture. Living in exile, Christians are to be "exemplary aliens" in the larger culture around them. They are to "forge for themselves an identity that sets them apart without necessarily setting them in conflict with the pagans around them."[43]

The positions described here have been labeled "a middle way," "social non-conformity," "social conformity," "identity and approval," "responsible investment," "participation without compromise," and "exemplary aliens." Although some overlap with others, they would seem to retain distinctive nuances. It is interesting that none of these interpretations of 1 Peter advocates a complete withdrawal of Christians from secular society. None, on the other hand, promotes a program of thoroughgoing transformation of society.

The Spirits in Prison and the Dead

During the past half-century, scholars have also turned their attention to two of the most difficult verses in 1 Peter, 3:19 and 4:6. The first relates that Christ "went and preached to the spirits in prison" (RSV). The second says that "the gospel was preached even to the dead" (RSV). **Bo Reicke** and **William J. Dalton** have advocated the two major ways of understanding these passages.

Reicke's interpretation, published in 1946, focuses on the positive theme of offering salvation to the sinful. He believes that the "spirits" in 3:19 are the fallen angels and also the souls of people from the time of Noah. The "prison" is in the underworld. Christ's preaching to the "spirits in prison," Reicke holds, occurred in connection with his descent to the underworld during the time between his death and resurrection.[44]

Reicke argues that the verb in 3:19 means specifically to proclaim the good news of the Christian gospel. When Christ was in the underworld, he proclaimed the secret about himself as the suffering and victorious Messiah. In this way he brought the possibility of conversion and salvation to sinners, both angelic and human, from times past.[45]

To relate 3:19 to its context, Reicke employs an argument "from a greater case to a lesser" *(a maiore ad minus)*. Just as Christ preached the gospel to the spirits of long ago, Christians should be prepared to speak courageously about their faith, even to those who are persecuting them. In this sense Reicke finds a clear missionary purpose in 1 Peter.[46]

Reicke believes that 4:6 addresses the same topic as 3:19. Referring to Christ's descent to the underworld, 4:6 signifies that the dead hear the gospel preached by Christ so that they can face final judgment. In this way the gospel shall be preached to all beings, or as many as possible, including the dead, while there is still time.[47]

With occasional variations in detail, a number of other scholars also understand 3:19 and 4:6 as references to Christ's preaching the gospel in the underworld. These include **Hans Windisch, Archibald M. Hunter,** and **Norman Hillyer.** "If we ask what value this tradition has for us today," Hunter comments, "the answer is that wherever men are, Christ has power to save."[48]

In 1965, **William J. Dalton** published an entirely different interpretation of the passage in 1 Peter containing 3:19 and 4:6. In 1989, he issued a revised edition of his study. References here are to the original publication, except where it is appropriate to refer to the revised edition.

Dalton understands 3:18–19 as a reference to the resurrection and ascension of Christ. The key phrase, "made proclamation to the spirits in prison," signifies Christ's proclamation of victory over hostile angelic powers in the course of his ascension. This proclamation is equivalent to the Pauline idea of the subjection of the powers and principalities, which is echoed in 3:22.[49]

In the revised edition of 1989, Dalton interprets the "proclamation of victory" in slightly different terms. Instead of emphasizing Christ's victory over, and condemnation of, the spiritual powers, he now understands 3:19 more in terms of "Christ's self-presentation as risen Lord to the hostile angelic powers in the heavens on the occasion of his ascension." Dalton continues to speak, however, in terms of Christ's "victory" over spiritual powers of evil.[50]

As Dalton understands 4:6, it refers to the "normal preaching of the gospel" to Christians who received the gospel during their lives on earth and then died; the background is that of 1 Thessalonians 4:13–18. The function of 4:6 is to counter the apparent futility of preaching to those who die before the Parousia.[51]

In both editions of his study, Dalton emphasizes that the purpose of the whole section, 3:18—4:6, is to provide a basis for encouraging Christians facing persecution. "Christ's victory over the powers of evil," he writes, "means the Christian's victory over the same powers and their earthly representatives."[52]

A number of recent interpreters, while recognizing the difficulty of the passage 3:18—4:6, tend to agree with Dalton's interpretation. These include **Edward G. Selwyn, Joseph A. Fitzmyer, John H. Elliott, Paul J. Achtemeier,** and **David L. Bartlett.**[53]

Major Topics and Concerns

As a final topic for further analysis, this survey may point to the problem of defining the purpose of 1 Peter. In a very general sense, it would seem that the letter seeks to confirm Christians in their faith and provide encouragement as they face persecution. Specialists differ, however, in identifying the strategies that the letter presents for achieving this goal.

According to **John H. Elliott,** 1 Peter encourages its readers to address their condition in society by resisting pressures for conformity. According to **David L. Balch,** the letter advises them to accept some degree of acculturation to the values of Hellenistic society as a way of finding acceptance in a non-Christian environment. Other scholars offer somewhat divergent interpretations of the relation of Christians to society. All these views contribute to the challenge of understanding the meaning of 1 Peter for today.

Interpretations of the difficult passage 3:18—4:6 also have their significance for Christians today. As **Bo Reicke** understands this section, Christ's offering of salvation to the inhabitants of the underworld provides an example for Christians to emulate, so that they adopt a missionary strategy and speak courageously about their faith to their secular neighbors. As **William J. Dalton** interprets 3:19, Christ's victory over the principalities and powers assures believers that they share, even now, in the ultimate triumph of good over evil. These believers, Dalton emphasizes, seek to endure in suffering rather than develop a missionary program.

As this summary suggests, these ways of identifying the main concerns and strategies of 1 Peter represent divergent approaches and interpretive stances. As a group, they testify to the complexity of the letter and the value of continuing study and analysis.

3
2 Peter

The letters of 2 Peter and Jude have a close literary relationship, since most of the verses in Jude have parallels in 2 Peter. Readers may wish, therefore, to look at the chapters on 2 Peter and Jude together. This chapter will focus on 2 Peter, treating issues of authorship and date, sources and affinities, occasion and setting, genre and structure, and major characteristics and concerns.

Authorship and Date

During the period covered by this book, most interpreters have supported the theory that 2 Peter is pseudonymous — that is, a later writer composed the letter in the name of the apostle Peter sometime between the end of the first century and the middle of the second. These interpreters often describe 2 Peter as the latest of the New Testament writings.

Albert E. Barnett has given perhaps the most extensive list of reasons supporting this view. He notes 1) that the reference to Jesus' prophecy of Peter's martyrdom (1:14) suggests an acquaintance with John 21. This in turn points to a knowledge of the four gospels as a published collection, since John 21 was probably written when the four gospels were issued together about 125 CE. 2) The writer of 2 Peter knows the tradition that the Gospel according to Mark was essentially Peter's (1:15).

3) The author assumes that his readers are familiar with the synoptic account of the Transfiguration (1:17). 4) The writer of 2 Peter incorporates Jude as his second chapter, and he is also clearly acquainted with 1 Peter (2:1–3:1). 5) The author's severe attitude toward backsliders (2:20–21) could reflect familiarity with the similar attitude of the writer of Hebrews (cf. Heb 6:4–8; 10:26–31).

6) Further, the writer implicitly includes himself with a generation that looks back on "the fathers" as figures of the past (3:4 [RSV]). 7) The writer knows Paul's letters as a published collection, and he reveres them along with "the other scriptures" (3:16). 8) The heretics who twist Paul's letters "to their own destruction" (3:16) could well be followers of Marcion (about 144 CE).[1]

Other commentators repeat a number of Barnett's arguments, and they also propose relatively late dates for 2 Peter. These include **J. Christiaan Beker, Bo Reicke, Thomas W. Leahy, Claude H. Thompson, Richard J. Bauckham, John H. Elliott, Pheme Perkins,** and **Duane F. Watson.** Collectively, these interpreters support Barnett's general position, and they also have individual emphases of their own.

Beker emphasizes that the author's purpose is to assure his readers that the Parousia will indeed occur.[2] Reicke believes that the positive attitude toward government fits in well with the political situation at about 90 CE.[3] Leahy believes that 2 Peter is "probably pseudonymous," and he suggests that the false teachers mentioned in the letter are "forerunners of various Christian Gnostics."[4] Thompson agrees with Barnett that the heretics could be followers of Marcion.[5]

Bauckham thinks that the writer of 2 Peter may be an "erstwhile colleague of Peter's," a member of a Petrine "circle" in Rome, writing about 80–90 CE and employing the testament form to represent the authority of the Roman church and its foremost leader.[6] Elliott calls attention to the writer's familiarity with Hellenistic rhetoric, apocalyptic traditions, the letter of Jude, and unidentified letters of Paul.[7] Perkins also notes that the author is well versed in the conventions of Hellenistic argument.[8]

Watson suggests that the author of 2 Peter is a strongly Hellenized Jewish Christian, from an urban setting, highly literate in Greek, and skilled in Greco-Roman rhetoric. Like Bauckham, he believes the author may belong to a Roman Petrine "circle," consisting of close associates and disciples of Peter.[9]

Although most scholars regard 2 Peter as a later, pseudonymous writing, **Norman Hillyer** takes very seriously the indications that the apostle Peter wrote the letter (1:1, 14–15, 16–18). Recognizing that no clear decision is possible, he finds six reasons to support apostolic authorship.

Hillyer begins 1) by questioning the idea of pseudonymous authorship, arguing there is little evidence that in ancient times personal letters were often published under assumed names. 2) The early church was very careful to check the authenticity of writings claiming to be apostolic. 3) Writers falsely claiming apostolic authority usually sought to promote some heresy. There is no suggestion, however, that the author of 2 Peter advocated heretical teachings.

Hillyer continues 4) by suggesting that the similarity of ideas between 1 Peter and 2 Peter can indicate that the same person wrote both letters. Also, 5) the reference to the death of "the fathers" (3:4) does not necessarily indicate a late date, since it refers more naturally to Old Testament figures than early Christian leaders. Finally, 6) 2 Peter alone in the New Testament mentions the destruction of the world by fire (3:12). Although this is sometimes understood as evidence of a late date, Hillyer notes that the theme is already present in the Thanksgiving Hymns (1QH 3:29–35) of the Dead Sea Scrolls.[10]

The preponderance of scholarly opinion, however, clearly supports the theory that a later writer composed 2 Peter in the name of the apostle Peter. It is intriguing, at the same time, to observe how carefully Hillyer weighs the possibilities for apostolic authorship.

Sources and Affinities

This section will be concerned primarily with the question whether 2 Peter used Jude as a source. It should be noted in this connection that 2 Peter is more than twice as long as Jude.

The question of the relationship between the two letters arises because Jude 4–13 has parallels in 2 Peter 2:1–18, and Jude 16–18 has parallels in 2 Peter 3:1–3. The parallels tend to be approximate rather than exact, but they are sufficiently close that they require some explanation.

Four theories are possible to explain these parallels. The most popular is that 2 Peter employed Jude as a source. A second explanation, the reverse of the first, is that Jude borrowed its material from 2 Peter. A third view is that the two letters made use of a common source. A fourth theory, seldom advocated, is that the same author wrote both letters.

Thomas W. Leahy gives a general logical argument to support the view that 2 Peter used Jude as a source. A priori, he believes, it is more likely that the longer epistle (2 Peter) has incorporated the shorter (Jude) than that the short one has abridged the longer.[11]

Similarly, **Richard J. Bauckham** notes that although much of Jude appears in 2 Peter, Jude's specific midrashic structure and exegetical techniques do not. It is easier, he believes, to imagine the writer of 2 Peter discarding these features in Jude than to think of the author of Jude constructing his complex Midrash from material in 2 Peter.[12]

In addition to these rather general arguments, **J. Christiaan Beker** gives some specific reasons for believing that 2 Peter utilized Jude. He notes, for example, that the sequence of events in 2 Peter 2:4–10 (involving angels, the Flood, and Sodom and Gomorrah) improves on the chronology of the incidents in Jude 5–7 (the Exodus, angels, and Sodom and Gomorrah).

Beker also calls attention to a theological alteration in 2 Peter 2:4–10. This passage describes the punishment of the wicked long ago, but it also introduces and emphasizes the redemption of the righteous (Noah with seven others, Lot). In contrast, the source in Jude 5–7 describes only the punishment of the wicked.[13]

Other interpreters who support the view that 2 Peter makes use of Jude include **Albert E. Barnett, John H. Elliott, Jerome H. Neyrey, Pheme Perkins,** and **Duane F. Watson.**[14] It would appear that this theory clearly represents the majority opinion concerning the relationship between the two letters.

In theory, it is possible to argue that the author of Jude draws most of his material from 2 Peter. Although earlier commentators occasionally sought to maintain this view, recent interpreters do not seem interested in promoting it.[15] The reasons for supporting 2 Peter's use of Jude also function, of course, as arguments against Jude's use of 2 Peter.

Another possibility is that the authors of 2 Peter and Jude draw independently from a common source. At least two recent commentators suggest this solution. **Bo Reicke** thinks in terms of a common oral tradition, possibly a "sermonic pattern," whereas **Norman Hillyer** envisages a written source.

Reicke and Hillyer emphasize that the writers of 2 Peter and Jude both have ideas of their own and sometimes treat their materials differently. They believe that the theory of a common source best accounts for the differences, as well as the parallels, between the two letters.[16] The issue here is partly a question concerning the relative importance of the similarities and the differences. Interpreters who believe the similarities outweigh the differences are more inclined to the explanation that 2 Peter makes use of Jude.[17]

The theory of common authorship represents a fourth possible explanation for the similarities between 2 Peter and Jude. During the period covered by this book, there do not appear to be any commentators who have advocated this view.

Richard J. Bauckham mentions this theory but gives two reasons for regarding it as implausible. He calls attention, first, to differences in style and background—that is, the Hellenistic nature of 2 Peter, and the Palestinian Jewish character of Jude. He also considers it unlikely that a writer would use his own work in the way 2 Peter uses Jude. The author of 2 Peter, for example, omits Jude's story of Michael's dispute with the devil, and also Jude's references to Cain and Korah.[18]

Occasion and Setting

This section treats the provenance and destination of 2 Peter, the identity of the "false teachers" among the addressees (2:1), and the cultural, philosophical, and religious milieu of the letter.

Since 2 Peter gives no indication of the place of writing or the intended destination, many commentators do not try to identify these venues. **Albert E. Barnett,** however, believes the letter may have been written in Rome as a general epistle intended for any Christians who might read it.

Barnett cites several factors pointing to Rome as the place of composition. These include the writer's abhorrence of heresy, his irenic picture of the relations between Peter and Paul, his allusion to Peter's death (1:14), the suggestion that Peter collaborated with Paul in instructing the churches by means of letters (3:1, 15), the reference to Mark's Gospel (1:15), and the influence of 1 Peter and Jude—both Roman documents—on the author of 2 Peter.

Barnett believes that the author composed a general letter for all Christians. "Its readers were any and all Christians," he writes, "to whose attention the little homily might come."[19]

John H. Elliott also suggests several factors that point to Rome as the place of origin: it was the site of Peter's death and the location of the "Petrine circle" that produced 1 Peter; affinities between 2 Peter and *1* and *2 Clement* and the *Shepherd of Hermas* suggest reliance on a common Roman tradition; these documents reflect a pastoral concern on the part of Roman Christians for other churches.

As the most likely destination for 2 Peter, Elliott believes that the evidence points to Asia Minor. Here pagan, Jewish, and Christian cultures came together, Epicureans were established, Paul's letters were collected, and another letter of Peter was known.[20]

From another point of view—sociological rather than geographical—**Jerome H. Neyrey** seeks to reconstruct the "social location" of the author of 2 Peter. This approach provides an intriguing alternative to the usual understanding of a concept such as "place."

The writer, Neyrey suggests, is a male who engages in typical male behavior, such as challenge/riposte exchanges, public association with other males, and paternal care of the group. The writer wishes to be honored as an elder whose word is authoritative. He is a male of the city, with literary and rhetorical skills, formally educated in Jewish and Christian traditions, and familiar with some Greek traditions. The author, Neyrey believes, makes a bicultural appeal to educated Jews and Greeks alike.[21]

During the period covered by this book, interpreters have suggested several ways of identifying the "false teachers" (2:1) who bring in "destructive opinions" (2:1), practice "licentious ways" (2:2), and scoff at the idea of the Parousia (3:3–4).

Bo Reicke understands the "false teachers" with reference to the Roman custom of *ambulatio*—that is, the practice of hiring officers of religious and social organizations to promote political and social propaganda. Certain men of the senatorial class are evidently employing church leaders to enlist the support of Christians for a revolt against the emperor Domitian. These church leaders, Reicke asserts, are the "false teachers" the writer of *2 Peter* condemns.[22]

As ingenious as this "political" theory is, it has evidently found no support among other interpreters of 2 Peter. Elliott refers to the theory but maintains that it has no basis in the text. Similarly, Neyrey states that he finds "no mention of the world of the Roman empire..." in the letter.[23] Those who wish to support this view must, it appears, re-examine the text for convincing references to the political situation in the Roman Empire under Domitian.

In contrast to **Bo Reicke,** several interpreters propose that the false teachers were Gnostics. **Albert E. Barnett,** followed by **Claude H. Thompson,** believes that they could well be followers of Marcion, about the middle of the second century. Others, such as **Thomas W. Leahy** and **George Eldon Ladd,** describe them more generally as Gnostics of some type.[24]

More recently, interpreters have questioned the identification of the false teachers as Gnostics. **Richard J. Bauckham,** in particular, argues there is no evidence in 2 Peter that these teachers subscribed to the cosmological dualism that is basic to gnosticism. Their background was pagan, and they expressed skepticism about the Parousia and eschatological judgment, but these characteristics would not make them Gnostics.[25]

Elliott and Neyrey both understand the false teachers as advocates of the type of rationalistic skepticism associated with Epicureanism. The teachers evidently reject ideas of divine involvement in human affairs, afterlife, and postmortem judgment. To counter this skepticism, the author of 2 Peter presents an apology defending divine judgment (3:9; 2:3b–9; 3:7, 9–13), afterlife (3:7, 10–13), and postmortem retribution (2:4, 9, 17; 3:7, 10).[26]

In her own study of 2 Peter, **Pheme Perkins** qualifies the belief that the author was opposing Epicurean arguments against divine judgment, providence, or justice. These arguments, she holds, appeared widely in philosophies of the time and were not necessarily Epicurean. Perkins believes, however, that 2 Peter clearly deals with the encounter between Christian faith and popular philosophy.[27]

As these references to Epicureanism and popular philosophies suggest, a number of interpreters situate 2 Peter in a Hellenistic cultural environment. The author and his audience, Elliott suggests, were both "at home in a pluralistic Hellenistic society."

Elliott gives a number of examples of the writer's acquaintance with Hellenistic thought: the list of Greek virtues (1:5–7); the description of death as a "putting off of the bodily tent" (1:13–14); the reference to the realm of the dead as "Tartarus" (2:4); interest in knowledge as a means of access to God (1:2, 3, 6, 8, 12; 2:20, 21; 3:3, 17, 18); the understanding of salvation as godliness (1:3), escape from corruption (1:4; 2:20), and participation in divine being (1:4).[28]

Genre and Structure

In this section, we discuss the literary category of "testament" that 2 Peter illustrates, the rhetorical conventions that it exhibits, and the "public inscription model" that it reflects. Many commentators describe 2 Peter as a testament or farewell address, supposedly presenting the last words of the apostle Peter. **Bo Reicke** lists other familiar examples of this genre: the *Testaments of the Twelve Patriarchs,* Jesus' farewell speech (John 13–17), Paul's farewell to the Ephesian elders (Acts 20:17–38), and 2 Timothy. **John H. Elliott** notes that this form allows the writer of 2 Peter to address current problems through the technique of giving reminders of the past and warnings of things to come. **Richard J. Bauckham** emphasizes that he regards 2 Peter as a genuine letter as well as a farewell speech.[29]

Among recent commentators, **Duane F. Watson,** in particular, has argued that the author of 2 Peter is a highly educated person familiar with the art of Greco-Roman rhetoric. As Watson understands the letter, 2 Peter is predominantly deliberative rhetoric, seeking to persuade its audience to do what is "advantageous, necessary, and expedient." The letter also contains sections of judicial rhetoric, involving accusation and defense (1:16—2:10a; 3:1–13), and epideictic rhetoric, expressing praise and blame (2:10b–22).[30]

Watson also analyzes 2 Peter from the standpoint of rhetorical components. These include the *exordium,* which makes contact with the audience and introduces the reasons for writing (1:3–11); the *probatio,* which offers proofs to support the reasons for the letter (1:16—3:13), and includes, in this instance, a *digressio* denouncing the false teachers (2:10b–22); and the *peroratio,* which summarizes the main points and appeals to the audience to respond as desired (3:14–16).[31]

Approaching 2 Peter from a different standpoint, **Frederick W. Danker** calls attention to the stereotyped language and style of public inscriptions celebrating the virtues and accomplishments of saviors and benefactors. Danker believes that the writer of 2 Peter intentionally composed the opening section (1:1–11) to create the effect of public decrees concerning benefactors and the recipients of their benefactions.

The author of 2 Peter, Danker writes, "found the decretal language about benefactors and recipients of benefactions well suited to express the reciprocity between Jesus as donor of salvation and Christians as recipients of forgiveness and power for new existence, now and in the age to come."[32] Danker's study of these parallels between public inscriptions and the opening section of 2 Peter provides a stimulating example of the application of cultural language patterns to the elucidation of a biblical text.

Major Characteristics and Concerns

This section focuses on questions of early Catholicism and 2 Peter's relevance for today. When commentators discuss the question of early Catholicism in 2 Peter, they often refer to an article by **Ernst Kaesemann** that was originally published in 1952 and appeared in English translation in 1964. Kaesemann severely criticizes 2 Peter for its supposed advocacy of early Catholicism. The letter, he argues, "is from beginning to end a document expressing an early Catholic viewpoint and is perhaps the most dubious writing in the canon."[33]

As evidence for early Catholicism, Kaesemann argues that 2 Peter understands "faith" as the Christian doctrinal tradition received from the apostles and now entrusted to the church; similarly, it regards "revelation" as virtually equivalent to the Christian religion. The letter's eschatology lacks a christological orientation, expressing instead the hope for individual participation in the divine nature on the basis of a Hellenistic dualism. Ethics is no longer the obedience of faith, effected by the Spirit, but a morality that seeks escape from the world of corruption. The church is now the possessor not only of correct doctrine, but of correct interpretation of scripture.[34]

Kaesemann's criticism of 2 Peter appears to have found few, if any, supporters. **Richard J. Bauckham** argues that the criticism fails because 2 Peter does have a vivid expectation of an imminent Parousia, does not appeal to ecclesiastical authorities, and does not assume a formalized creedal orthodoxy. **Duane F. Watson** supports these arguments, noting in particular that the author expects the recipients of the letter to be alive when the Parousia occurs.[35]

Jerome H. Neyrey addresses the criticism that 2 Peter's eschatology lacks a christological orientation. If the letter seems to lack a christological focus, Neyrey argues, it is not because the author was an early Catholic. The author was addressing a specific attack on theodicy, not Christology. "The issue," Neyrey emphasizes, "was divine judgment in general, not Christ's in particular."[36]

George Eldon Ladd disagrees with Kaesemann's argument that the author's world view rests on Hellenistic dualism, involving the contrast between imprisonment in the world of passion and participation in the divine nature (1:4). If this is true, Ladd replies, "the epistle has adopted the basic world view of the very Gnostic heresy it is refuting." Ladd argues further that participation in the divine nature does not mean apotheosis, but seems to refer to the present experience of Christian life—that is, the gift of the Spirit of God and of sonship.[37]

Although many interpreters seek to explain the relevance of 2 Peter for today, perhaps **John H. Elliott** has addressed this issue most cogently and effectively. The concerns of 2 Peter, he writes, "retain perennial significance. For when skeptics of any age question the rule of God in human history, the certainty of afterlife, Christ's coming in power and judgment, and the implications of this for Christian morality, then this recollection of the ancient apostolic tradition assumes fresh urgency and vitality."[38]

4
1 John

Because the three letters of John are similar in language, style, and content, this chapter begins with a discussion of general issues of authorship and date related to the study of all three letters. The chapter then focuses more specifically on 1 John, treating questions of sources and affinities, occasion and setting, genre and structure, and major characteristics and concerns. As in the treatment of the previous Catholic Epistles, this chapter seeks to identify, wherever possible, broad areas of agreement or trends in interpretation.

Authorship and Date

In his 1957 commentary, **Amos N. Wilder** advocated the view that all three letters of John have a common author and illuminate each other. The "elder" or "presbyter" wrote 1 John as well as 2 and 3 John, although he did not identify himself in this way in 1 John.

This unknown author, Wilder believes, wrote the three letters during the first decade of the second century, addressing churches in the Roman province of Asia that were struggling with issues raised by Gnosticism and Docetism. The letters reflect a period when responsible leaders were seeking to establish norms for faith, conduct, and fellowship based on revelation that was "from the beginning" (1 John 1:1).[1]

Wilder also believes that the author of 1 John was different from the author of the Gospel of John. He cites a number of differences that require this conclusion. First John, for example, makes almost no reference to the Old Testament. It does not "spiritualize" the ideas of the Second Coming and the Last Judgment. It identifies Jesus himself with the Paraclete, who will offer intercession in heaven.[2]

In contrast to Wilder, **George B. Caird** regards the authorship of the three letters as very much an open question. Although he does not argue for any particular solution, he considers three theories, which he designates the Muratorian, the "traditional," and the Hieronymian.

The Fragment theory holds that 1 and 2 John are by one author and 3 John by another. This view rests on the negative evidence of Irenaeus (toward the end of the second century CE) and the Muratorian Fragment (ca. 200 CE), which make no mention of 3 John. A problem with this view, Caird notes, is that 2 and 3 John both claim to be written by the "elder" or "presbyter," and it is difficult to think that either one imitated the other.

The "traditional" theory is that John the Apostle wrote the Gospel of John and all three letters of John. This view, Caird points out, would make it necessary to identify John the Apostle with John the Elder (or Presbyter), who wrote 2 and 3 John.

The Hieronymian theory, favored by Jerome, is that John the Apostle wrote the gospel and 1 John, and John the Elder wrote 2 and 3 John. Jerome could not believe that the apostle would have referred to himself merely as "presbyter" or "elder." One problem with this view, Caird suggests, is that the apostolic authorship of 1 John rests solely on its opening sentence, with its claim to eyewitness evidence. This sentence may refer, however, to the corporate experience of the church rather than the individual experience of the writer.[3]

Emphasizing the close literary relations among the Johannine writings, **Bruce Vawter** proposes a variant of the traditional theory of authorship. He regards it as "virtually certain" that "the same secretary-disciple of John the Apostle" wrote the gospel and the three letters of John. Vawter believes that the materials in the gospel passed through a period of oral history before it received its present written form. In a broad sense, 1 John can be considered a commentary on the traditions taught in the Johannine school.[4]

Massey H. Shepherd Jr. and **Pheme Perkins** offer similar variants of the traditional theory. Shepherd considers it likely that the "editor" who shaped the Gospel of John also wrote 1 John and probably 2 and 3 John. Perkins suggests that a disciple of the "evangelist" (the author of the Gospel of John) gave the gospel its final form after the evangelist died, and this disciple may have written the Johannine letters as well.[5]

Although he recognizes the close affinity in language and content between 1 John and the Gospel of John, **Rudolf Bultmann** maintains that they were written by different persons. The decisive argument, he holds, is that they are directed at different fronts—the gospel is directed to the "world," that is, non-Christians, whereas 1 John seeks to counteract the views of false teachers who claim to represent the genuine Christian faith. This difference indicates that the gospel is earlier than 1 John.[6]

Raymond E. Brown also emphasizes that the gospel and letters of John contend with different opponents. In the gospel, the Johannine community is engaged in debate with five outside groups—the "Jews" of the synagogue who expelled the Johannine Christians, crypto-Christians who remain in the synagogues without publicly confessing their faith in Jesus, followers of John the Baptist who regard him as God's prime emissary, Jewish Christians who confess Jesus as the Messiah but do not consider him divine, and Christians of the "Apostolic Churches" who consider themselves heirs of the Twelve and recognize the divinity of Jesus but apparently not his pre-existence.[7]

In the Gospel of John, the Johannine community engages representatives of these outside groups. None of the groups, Brown believes, seems to have so high a Christology—especially in terms of pre-existence—as the Johannine community itself.

The letters of John do not have any of these outside groups in mind. They contend, rather, with former insiders who have left the community—that is, the secessionists. Thus the letters address a different situation from that envisaged in the gospel.[8]

Brown thinks of four persons as involved in the composition of the gospel and the letters: the Beloved Disciple (the source of the Johannine community's traditions about Jesus and the authority for many of its theological insights), the evangelist (the writing author of the gospel), the presbyter (author of the epistles), and the final redactor of the Gospel. Brown does not try to give names to these four figures.[9] In relation to this process of composition, he believes one person was the author of the Gospel of John, and another of the epistles.[10]

With regard to dates, Brown believes that the Gospel of John took shape over a period of several decades, involving accumulation of traditions about Jesus, selecting and rewriting of the traditions into a basic gospel, and final additions by a redactor after the evangelist's death. He thinks that the "pre-Gospel Johannine community history" extended from the mid-50s to the 80s; the body of the gospel was written about 90; and the final redaction was just after 100.

With regard to the epistles, Brown believes that 1 John was written about 100; 2 John, close in time to 1 John; and 3 John between 100 and 110. First John was probably addressed to the main church community in Ephesus, and 2 and 3 John to Johannine house-churches in outlying towns.[11]

Robert Kysar treats the question of authorship in much the same way as **Raymond Brown.** Like Brown, he speaks of Johannine tradition and a Johannine community that produced the gospel and the letters. Like Brown, he believes that the letters are sufficiently different from the gospel that they must come from a different author. Like Brown also, Kysar believes 2 and 3 John were written by the same person, the elder or presbyter.[12]

Kysar differs from Brown in emphasizing the differences between 1 John and the other letters. First John, he notes, does not identify its author as the "elder." It reveals a far more poetic style than the others. It does not reflect the more developed view of the church and its authority structure found in 2 and 3 John. For reasons such as these, Kysar thinks in terms of separate authorship for 1 John. He notes at the same time that the similarities among the three letters argue for an origin in a single community.[13]

In establishing dates for the Johannine writings, Kysar notes that several developments seem to have occurred between the writing of the gospel and the publication of the letters: 1) The Johannine community has recovered from its expulsion from the synagogue, the event that occasioned the production of the gospel. The community is not concerned now with external opponents but with an internal problem. 2) The community has, to some degree, integrated other Christian perspectives into its own beliefs (e.g., the idea of expiation, 1 John 2:2). 3) The community has a stronger tendency to think in terms of proper doctrine (2 John 9). 4) Some "unofficial organizational structure" has emerged, so that the terms "church" (3 John 6, 9, 10) and "elder" have come into use.[14]

In light of these developments, Kysar concludes that the epistles could have been written about a decade after the Gospel of John—that is, from 90 to 105 CE, depending on the date given to the gospel. Kysar thinks in terms of a Syrian locale for the gospel and the letters.[15]

Other recent commentators also represent this general view that one author wrote the Gospel of John, and one or two others produced the letters. These include **D. Moody Smith, Rudolf Schnackenburg, Georg Strecker,** and **C. Clifton Black.**[16] Like Vawter, Brown, and Kysar, recent commentators frequently speak of a school, circle, or community that preserved Johannine tradition and produced the Johannine writings over a period of some years.

Sources and Affinities

Some scholars have argued that the writer of 1 John utilized a written source. The first person to propose this hypothesis was evidently **Ernst von Dobschuetz,** who argued in 1907 that 1 John 2:28 — 3:12 was an elaboration of a brief original "composition." He identified and arranged this source as follows:

> Every one who does right is born of him (2:29b)
> Every one who commits sin is guilty of lawlessness (3:4)
>   No one who abides in him sins (3:6a)
>   No one who sins has seen him (3:6b)
> He who does right is righteous (3:7b)
> He who commits sin is of the devil (3:8a)
>   No one born of God commits sin (3:9a)
>   No one who does not do right is of God (3:10b [author's translation])[17]

Von Dobschuetz noted that the source consisted of four pairs of lines, each pair showing antithetical parallelism. He also called attention to close correspondences between the first and third pairs, and the second and fourth. Von Dobschuetz suggested that the terse, lapidary style, with its absence of connectives, reflected a Semitic way of thinking. In a similar way he argued that the content of the source, with its emphasis on ethical concepts, was reminiscent of the perspective of ancient Israel.[18]

Twenty years later, **Rudolf Bultmann** presented his own independent study of a hypothetical source underlying 1 John. With the help of some reconstructed words and lines, he identified a more extensive source that included most of the material von Dobschuetz had isolated but drew some verses from every chapter in the letter. At this time Bultmann's source consisted of 26 pairs of lines from 1 John and one pair from 2 John.[19]

In contrast to von Dobschuetz, Bultmann assigned the source to the category of "revelation discourse." It was of "oriental" origin, and its style reflected the viewpoint of "a cosmological and religious dualism."[20] The author of 1 John, Bultmann believed, elaborated on this source with homiletical exposition, references to earlier tradition, and paraenetical admonition.[21]

Bultmann continued to maintain his hypothesis of a written source in 1 John, stylistically related to the Revelation Discourses source that he posited for the Gospel of John. In his 1973 commentary, he again gave the text of the source for 1 John. Apart from some modifications, this version was essentially the same as the one that he reconstructed in 1927. The main difference was that he now arranged much of the material in stanzas of three lines, rather than two.[22]

In an article originally published in 1951 and reprinted in 1967, Bultmann added a kind of codicil to his theory by proposing that certain parts of 1 John derive from later ecclesiastical redaction rather than the original author or his source. In particular, he singled out 5:14–21 as a later addition, arguing that it had no connection to the preceding ideas. He was also critical of certain verses reflecting a futurist eschatology (2:28; 3:2; 4:17) or depicting atonement through Jesus' death (1:7b; 2:2; 4:10b). Bultmann regarded these verses also as later interpolations.[23]

In his 1957 commentary, **Amos N. Wilder** accepted the theory that the author of 1 John utilized a written source arranged in couplets. In his own exposition he frequently referred to such a source.[24] Subsequent interpreters, however, have been much more critical. Some point to internal weaknesses in this theory, while others wish to emphasize the importance of oral tradition.

Raymond E. Brown criticizes the views of both von Dobschuetz and Bultmann. Regarding the theory of von Dobschuetz, he asks why, if such a source existed, the writer of 1 John sometimes broke up the lines of the couplets and why similar lines of the same style and ethical content were not assigned to the source.

With regard to Bultmann, Brown asks in a similar way why the author would break up a self-contained source, scattering verses all over 1 John (and even placing one in 2 John) and why Bultmann excluded Christian elements in reconstructing his source.[25]

With regard to the style of 1 John, Brown suggests that it has many antithetical statements, not because the writer was utilizing a written source, but because he was reporting and then responding to the views of his opponents.[26]

In a similar vein, **Rudolf Schnackenburg** calls attention to the frequent changes in style in 1 John. These result in part, he suggests, from the dual purpose of the document—it is a didactic-polemical writing directed against the heretics, and it is also a homiletical-paraenetic work addressed to the Johannine community.[27]

Pheme Perkins argues that stylistic and linguistic data are lacking to support the theory of a written source. She believes instead that the author of 1 John "has a variety of sources at his disposal, most of them oral in character." In this connection she emphasizes the importance of "the oral modes of cognition and authority that were still very much part of the world of the 1st and 2nd centuries." The author, she believes, uses traditional formulas and slogans, some of which derive from synoptic-like tradition that may have circulated freely in the Johannine church.[28]

With a similar emphasis on oral sources, **Georg Strecker** describes 1 John as a combination of letter and sermon. He sees it as a homily, addressed to the congregations that make up the community as a whole, cast in the form of a letter. Its various parts, Strecker believes, reflect ongoing discussions within the Johannine school.[29]

Occasion and Setting

During the period covered by this book, three specialists— **Raymond E. Brown, Robert Kysar,** and **Rudolf Schnackenburg**—have given close attention to the problem of identifying the false teachers the author of 1 John opposes. Although they do not reach definitive conclusions, their studies illumine the setting in which the writer of the letter seeks to help his readers understand and practice their Christian faith.

Brown notes that these teachers had belonged to the Johannine community but withdrew from it (1 John 2:19). They are probably not Jews, or lapsed Christian Jews, or Christians who overemphasize the humanity of Jesus. They are probably Christians whose Christology is "too high," stressing the pre-existence of Jesus to the point of neglecting his humanity. They evidently admit the reality of Jesus' humanity but deny the salvific value of his career in the flesh and the degree to which that career belonged to his identity as the Christ.[30]

Brown rejects any identification of the false teachers with the followers of Cerinthus, an early heretic active in the province of Asia around the end of the first century CE. Cerinthus proposed a form of Docetism that differentiated between the divine "Christ" and the human "Jesus." The divine Christ, he taught, descended upon the man Jesus at his baptism and then withdrew before Jesus suffered, died, and rose again.[31]

Brown calls attention especially to 1 John 5:6, which speaks of the coming of Jesus Christ in water and blood, with reference, presumably, to Jesus' baptism and then his death. Some interpreters, he notes, believe this verse is directed against the Cerinthians, on the grounds that it denies that the Christ was an impassible being who left Jesus before his death.

Brown sees difficulties in this interpretation. If the writer of 1 John is opposing Cerinthus, Brown asks whether he would not speak of the coming of Christ on Jesus, rather than the coming of Jesus Christ. Brown also asks whether the writer would not be making a partial concession to Cerinthus by speaking of the coming of Jesus Christ in water (i.e., at baptism).

For these reasons Brown refrains from identifying the adversaries in 1 John with Cerinthians. He believes 1 John 5:6 opposes "a Christological dualism which posited only a partial union between the divine and the human in Jesus Christ—a dualism less developed than that attributed to Cerinthus."[32]

Robert Kysar is especially concerned to describe the attitudes, beliefs, and activities of the false teachers, even if he cannot identify them with any specific party in the early church. He looks first for explicit references to them in the letter, and then for possible allusions that the author makes.

On the basis of explicit references, Kysar suggests that the false teachers do not practice love in their relationship with the readers (2:9–11; 4:20–21); do not acknowledge the humanity of the Christ (4:2–3; cf. 2:22; 5:5–6); have aligned themselves with "the world" (4:5–6); function as instruments of evil (3:8) and as anti-Christs (2:18–23); were never authentic Christians—that is, members of the Johannine community (2:19).

Kysar also thinks it likely that the author makes the following allusions to these separatists: they do not adhere to the teachings of the writer and/or the Christian community (4:6); they falsely claim to know and love God (2:4; 4:20) and to be in "the light" (1:6; 2:9); they are guilty of "mortal" sin (5:16); they falsely regard themselves as free of sin (1:6–10; 3:3–6); they do not recognize moral restrictions in their behavior (3:4–10).

Kysar is cautious about identifying the separatists with any group known from other sources. He notes that they probably hold a view of Christ that limits his human characteristics, and they do not practice a strict morality. He does not believe the evidence supports the view that they are "pure docetists and/or antinomians." He does think that they are very probably "predecessors of a later Gnostic Christianity."[33]

In a very similar way, **Rudolf Schnackenburg** suggests that the religious and ethical deviation of the false teachers "shows a Gnostic tendency." He also believes that these persons are to be sought predominantly in a Gentile Christian milieu.[34]

Schnackenburg argues further that the heresy combated in 1 John cannot simply be identified with the views of Cerinthus, although it has certain points of contact with them. He notes that 1) there is no distinction in this heresy between a supreme deity and an inferior deity, as there is in Cerinthus; 2) there is no differentiation between the spiritual Christ and the man Jesus, as there is in Cerinthus; 3) the heretics in 1 John deny the incarnation for general reasons of Christology and soteriology, whereas Cerinthus denies it on the grounds that the virginal conception is incredible.

Schnackenburg argues further that 4) the heretical teachers in 1 John reject redemption in the blood of Jesus because they deny the whole Christian doctrine of salvation, while Cerinthus rejects it because he regards the spiritual Christ as impassible; and 5) the external evidence in Irenaeus, Epiphanius, and Jerome indicates only that the Gospel of John is directed against Cerinthus.[35]

A number of recent interpreters have proposed that the heretical teachers in 1 John were influenced in some way by the type of Docetism connected with the name of Cerinthus.[36] Brown, Kysar, and Schnackenburg, however, all refrain from giving a specific identity to these teachers. Brown and Schnackenburg emphasize that they cannot be seen simply as Cerinthians, while Kysar and Schnackenburg describe them more generally as tending toward Gnosticism.

Genre and Structure

Just as interpreters offer different perspectives on the identity of the false teachers in 1 John, they suggest different ways of analyzing the genre and structure of the writing. Some question whether 1 John is a genuine letter. Some focus on stylistic characteristics, such as repetition and antithesis. Others emphasize the importance of content, such as doctrine and paraenesis. Still others undertake, with varying results, to provide an outline for the writing.

Anos N. Wilder thinks of 1 John as a pastoral tractate carried by itinerant missionaries. He notes that it lacks an epistolary introduction, an explicit designation of its author, and a closing salutation. Yet 1 John, he believes, does have some marks of a letter. The writer visualizes his readers and their situation, and he addresses them directly with warmth and authority. He employs a paraenetic style marked by personal appeal, contrasts of right and wrong, and rhetorical questions.[37]

Wilder does not think that the outline of 1 John is entirely clear. He does suggest, however, that the earlier section is concerned with righteousness and obedience, the central part (especially 3:11—4:21) develops the theme of love, and the closing part deals with faith and confidence.[38] This observation would help first-time readers, in particular, identify major themes in the letter.

Massey H. Shepherd Jr. focuses on the literary device of antithesis, which appears so frequently in 1 John. He understands the letter as a "spiral" of contrasts, such as light/darkness, truth/lie, keeping the commandments/sin, love/hate, of the Father/of the world, the one from the beginning/the evil one.[39]

Understanding the letter in this way, readers would not necessarily look for logical development of thought. They would be attentive, instead, to the writer's technique of highlighting important concepts by contrasting them with their opposites.

Rudolf Bultmann analyzes the structure of 1 John with reference to his theories of an earlier source and a later redaction. He believes, for example, that the writer was using and commenting on his source in the major part of the letter, 1:1—5:13. Within this section, he regards 1:5—2:27 as originally an independent writing or rough draft, and describes 2:28—5:12 as a "compendium" of fragments representing sketches or meditations by the author or his disciples. Bultmann suggests that the proem in 1:1–4 imitates the prescript of a letter, 5:13 imitates the usual conclusion, and the appendix in 5:14–21 is a later addition.[40] Although Bultmann's analysis may seem unnecessarily complex, his attempt to correlate structure with source and redaction forces the reader to pay very close attention to the meaning of each part of the letter.

Pheme Perkins understands 1 John in relation to her emphasis on the importance of oral communication in the ancient world. The "formulaic and repetitive" nature of oral discourse, she believes, helps to explain the "theme-and-variations" pattern of the letter.[41] Like the "spiral" of contrasts that Shepherd described, the "theme-and-variations" pattern helps the reader identify prominent themes in the letter and establish their relation to one another.

Reflecting his theory of a Johannine community that produced several writings to address changing situations, **Raymond E. Brown** suggests that the author of 1 John used the Gospel of John as a model. Each document is divided into two parts. The first deals with the opponents that Christian believers must face — the secessionists in 1 John (1:5 — 3:10) and "the Jews" in the Gospel of John (2 — 12). The second part describes the revelation of divine love for believers in 1 John (3:11 — 5:12) and in the gospel (13–20). Both documents, that is, reflect an "outsiders/insiders" pattern.[42]

Robert Kysar believes, as Perkins argued earlier, that the repetitious style of 1 John betrays an origin in oral communication. Kysar suggests specifically that the author attempts to draw together parts of several homilies, delivered at different times, and direct them to the critical situation that the community is facing.

Kysar divides 1 John into nine sections, which may be fragments of homilies originating in the Johannine community: 1) Introduction: Christian Life and Fellowship (1:1–4); 2) Light and Darkness (1:5 — 2:11); 3) Believers and the World (2:12–17); 4) Truth and Life (2:18–29); 5) The Children of God and the Children of the Devil (3:1–24); 6) The Spirit of Truth and the Spirit of Error (4:1–6); 7) God's Love and the Believer's Love (4:7 — 5:5); 8) The Son and Witnesses to the Son (5:6–12); 9) Conclusion: Knowing and Doing (5:13–21).[43]

In much the same way as Perkins and Kysar, **Georg Strecker** finds the basis of 1 John in oral discourse. He understands it as a sermon, presented in the form of a letter, addressed to multiple congregations that make up the Johannine community. He also focuses on the content of the writing, differentiating between alternating sections of paraenesis and dogmatic exposition.

Following this approach, Strecker provides the following outline: prelude (1:1–4), paraenesis (1:5 — 2:17), dogmatic exposition (2:18–27), paraenesis (2:28 — 3:24), dogmatic exposition

(4:1–6), paraenesis (4:7 — 5:4a), dogmatic exposition (5:4b–12), and final paraenetic remarks (5:13–21). Strecker notes that the theme of conflict with opponents is restricted mainly to the dogmatic sections. The letter as a whole, he believes, expresses the author's affection for the Christian community rather than an interest in polemics.[44]

It is interesting to note that outlines of 1 John differ significantly from one another. Bultmann finds a major division after 2:27; Brown finds the major break after 3:10; in the middle of the letter, Kysar finds sections ending at 2:29 and 3:24; Strecker finds somewhat similar sections ending at 2:27 and 3:24; few of the sections that Kysar identifies coincide exactly with those in Strecker's outline. The task of providing a generally accepted outline for 1 John remains a continuing challenge.

Major Characteristics and Concerns

This section looks at some of the critical issues that become apparent in a study of 1 John. These include textual problems relating to the Muratorian Fragment and the "Johannine Comma," which is a gloss in 5:7–8 that introduces the idea of the Trinity. They also include questions concerning sinlessness, eschatology, "early Catholicism," and the theological achievement of the author.

Noted earlier in this chapter, **George B. Caird** described a "Muratorian theory" of authorship, which maintained that 1 and 2 John were by one writer and 3 John by another. This view rested on the negative evidence of Irenaeus and the Muratorian Fragment, which do not mention 3 John.

More recently, **Georg Strecker** has suggested that the Muratorian Fragment possibly refers to all three letters, although it does not acknowledge 2 and 3 John as genuine Johannine writings. The issue involves the interpretation of the vernacular Latin in which the Fragment is written.[45] Although the question remains open, it is important to notice that Strecker has called attention to this problem.

A further issue in the area of textual criticism concerns the "Johannine Comma" in 1 John 5:7–8. The purpose of this passage was evidently to explain the "three witnesses" in relation to the persons of the Trinity. The King James Version prints the "Johannine Comma" in brackets: "There are three that bear record [in heaven, the Father, the Word, and the Holy Ghost; and these three are one. And there are three that bear witness in earth], the spirit, and the water, and the blood; and these three agree in one."[46]

George B. Caird asserts there is "not the slightest doubt" that the words in brackets are an interpolation. He notes that they occur in only two late Greek manuscripts. They are not found in any ancient version except the Latin. They are absent from the Old Latin text used by Tertullian, Cyprian, and Augustine, and also from Jerome's Vulgate. The words were first quoted as part of 1 John by the Spanish heretic Priscillian, who died in 385. Later they were accepted into the Vulgate and eventually into the Complutensian Polyglot of 1514, the Textus Receptus, and the King James Version.[47]

Recent commentators would appear to be unanimous in agreeing with the judgment that Caird expressed. If the Johannine Comma was a well-intentioned attempt to understand a verse in terms of the Trinity, it must nevertheless be rejected on textual grounds. **Rudolf Schnackenburg** and **Georg Strecker,** in particular, give detailed accounts of the textual history of the passage. Schnackenburg also notes that an official pronouncement of the Holy Office, dated June 6, 1927, allowed Catholic scholars to regard the Johannine Comma as a later addition.[48]

Recent interpreters take different approaches to the question of sinlessness as it occurs in 1 John. The problem is that the writer seems to make different assertions about the possibility of sinlessness—that is, Christian believers do sin, but if they confess their sins, they can turn to God for forgiveness (1:8–10), and they also find forgiveness through Jesus (1:7; 2:1–2, 12; 4:10); those, on the other hand, who abide in God (3:6), or are born of God (3:9; 5:18), do not sin.

Willliam Barclay, Pheme Perkins, and D. Moody Smith illustrate three different approaches to the problem of sinlessness. Their solutions may be labeled grammatical, communal, and polemical, respectively. Although every commentator on 1 John must address this problem, these three solutions represent thoughtful, judicious attempts to resolve a complex issue.

Barclay notes the apparent contradiction between 1:8–10 (which promises that if believers confess their sins, God, who is faithful and just, will forgive their sins) and 3:9 (which asserts that those born of God do not commit sin). He deals with this inconsistency by calling attention to 2:1, in which the writer says he is writing "that you may not sin." Barclay notes that the verb "sin" here is aorist, denoting a "particular and definite act." In contrast, the statement in 3:9 uses the present tense for the idea of committing sin, indicating a habitual action.

Putting these verses together, Barclay believes the sense is that Christians may commit individual acts of sin, in spite of their serious efforts not to do so, but they can never become "deliberate and consistent" sinners. "John is not saying that the man who abides in God cannot sin," he concludes, "but he is saying that the man who abides in God cannot continue to be a deliberate sinner."[49]

Perkins approaches the issue of sinlessness in the context of her emphasis on the central importance of the community as the locus of fellowship, forgiveness, righteousness, and Christian love.[50] From this perspective, she argues that the references to sinfulness and forgiveness in 1:6, 8, and 2:1–2 are not inconsistent with the treatment of sinlessness in 3:4–10.

In Chapter 3, Perkins believes, the author is primarily concerned with "the holiness and righteousness of the community," which is possible despite the wrongs committed by individuals. Although the writer of 1 John declares in 3:9 that God's "seed" or "nature" abides in everyone born of God, Perkins argues that this metaphor is a group designation rather than an individual one. In this sense it is possible that sinlessness can characterize the Christian community.[51]

Like Barclay and Perkins, Smith recognizes the tension between the verses in 1 John that speak of sinfulness and those that apparently make a claim to sinlessness. He focuses especially on the assertion, "No one born of God commits sin" (3:9). Smith suggests that this may perhaps be a motto of the author's opponents, making a claim to moral perfection, which the author picks up and throws back at them. Thus the writer is concerned that Christians make every effort to avoid sin, but he is not thinking in terms of "a kind of born-again perfectionism."[52]

During the period covered by this book, interpreters have usually taken the position that the Gospel of John understands the significance of Jesus primarily in terms of realized eschatology, whereas 1 John puts more emphasis on a futurist eschatology. This is the case, for instance, with **Amos N. Wilder, Bruce Vawter, Raymond E. Brown,** and **Robert Kysar.**[53] Commentators seem to support this position generally, regardless of their views on the authorship or chronology of the two writings.

A notable exception is **Rudolf Bultmann,** who regards the expressions of futurist eschatology in the Gospel of John and 1 John as later ecclesiastical interpolations. First John, for example, speaks of the Parousia of Christ (2:28); it promises that believers will be "like him" when he appears (3:2); and it assures them that they can have "confidence for the day of judgment" (4:17 [RSV]). Bultmann assigns all three verses to the ecclesiastical redaction which, he believes, 1 John underwent. Elsewhere in 1 John also, he believes, futurist eschatology has been historicized.[54]

It is interesting to note that Bultmann treats the concepts of light and darkness in the same way he treats futurist eschatology. He points out that light and darkness are cosmic powers in Gnosticism, and Johannine dualism shares this terminology with Gnosticism. In the Gospel of John and 1 John, however, the cosmological dualism of Gnosticism has been historicized. The result is that "a dualism of decision arises out of the cosmological dualism," and "the decision of faith is the choice between two possibilities of self-understanding offered by the proclamation."[55] As these quotations indicate, Bultmann understands the phenomenon of historicization in terms of existentialist "decision" and "self-understanding."

A study by **Guenter Klein** also utilizes the categories of light and darkness as methodological concepts for analyzing the structure of eschatology in the Johannine writings. Turning first to the Gospel of John, he notes that light and darkness are "chronologically undifferentiated" with regard to the past, present, and future of world history. The author, Klein believes, is interested "only in the difference between light and darkness on the plane of existential time." It is only on this plane that the two powers stand in tension or meet in conflict.[56]

With regard to 1 John, Klein focuses especially on the statement in 2:8, "the darkness is passing away and the true light is already shining." This verse indicates, Klein argues, that a temporal relation exists between the two powers. Their reciprocal relationship is "chronologically differentiated, in the sense that the passing away of the darkness corresponds to the shining forth of the light." The light represents a new epoch that began with Christ and continues to come in a genuinely chronological sense.[57]

Klein's understanding of the ahistorical relation of light and darkness in the Gospel of John closely resembles Bultmann's existentialist interpretation. Klein's analysis of 1 John, however, situates light and darkness on a chronological continuum in which one decreases and the other increases. In this respect Klein would differ from Bultmann and would support the majority of interpreters, who argue that 1 John places more emphasis on a futurist eschatology.

Another major issue that arises in the study of 1 John is the possibility of "early Catholicism." Recent commentators seem to refrain from using this expression, even when they are dealing with issues that might possibly fall into this category. **Raymond E. Brown,** for example, approaches the topic by comparing the letters of John with the Gospel of John. He finds much truth in the view that the letters stand in relation to the gospel in the same way as the

Pastoral Epistles stand in relation to the earlier, undisputed letters of Paul.

In each case, Brown suggests, there is "a concretizing of insights, an appeal to tradition, a defensiveness against dangers from within, and a certain cautious retrenchment." He does not, however, apply the phrase "early Catholicism" to the Johannine letters, since 1 John reveals none of the emphasis on structure and authoritative teaching offices that is present in 1 and 2 Timothy and Titus.[58]

From a very similar perspective, **Robert Kysar** notes that the church at the end of the first century sought to clarify the meaning of authentic Christian faith as a way of acquiring an identity and preserving itself for the future. He suggests that 1 and 2 John contributed two vital aspects of this "emerging orthodoxy"—the centrality of the humanity of Christ and the importance of the moral dimension of Christian life.[59]

Referring to all three letters, Kysar observes that the Johannine community has to some degree integrated other Christian perspectives into its own beliefs (e.g., the idea of expiation, 1 John 2:2); the community has a stronger tendency to think in terms of proper doctrine (2 John 9); and some "unofficial organization structure" has emerged, so that the terms "church" (3 John 6, 9, 10) and "elder" have come into use.[60]

Although he uses expressions such as "emerging orthodoxy" and "unofficial organizational structure," Kysar, like Brown, refrains from speaking of "early Catholicism." Both scholars evidently believe that the developments occurring about the end of the first century were not yet sufficiently widespread or advanced to warrant use of this phrase.

A recent article by **C. Clifton Black** seeks to define "early Catholicism" in more detail and then apply this definition to the data in the Johannine epistles. Black himself regards his results as inconclusive. His study deserves attention, however, because it raises the question whether "early Catholicism" is an appropriate model for historical research.

Black begins by identifying twelve characteristics of early Catholicism: 1) a concern for transmission and interpretation of tradition; 2) an interest in collecting apostolic writings; 3) a distinction between laity and clergy; 4) a church organization that is basically hierarchical rather than charismatic; 5) the development of a monarchical episcopate; 6) a principle of transmission of authority, or apostolic succession; 7) a static, objective conception of faith, rather than a dynamic, subjective understanding; 8) an emphasis on sound doctrine ("orthodoxy"), as opposed to false teaching ("heresy"); 9) a moralization of faith, tending toward legalism; 10) a concern for ecclesiastical consolidation and unity; 11) a trend toward "sacramentalism," promoting a view of the church as the purveyor of salvation; 12) the waning of apocalyptic eschatology in general, and expectation of the Parousia in particular.[61]

Applying these criteria to 1, 2, and 3 John, Black indicates that he is "not persuaded that the Johannine epistles are *fundamentally* documents of 'early Catholicism,' as that term has been herein defined."[62] In these letters he notes, for example, that tradition is important, but also flexible and dynamic; there is no evident interest in a collection of apostolic writings; there is no discernible distinction between clergy and laity; ecclesial "organization" is principally charismatic rather than hierarchical; and the presbyter's authority is personal rather than official.

Faith, Black continues, is understood primarily as a subjective commitment (*fides qua creditur*) rather than a static body of dogma (*fides quae creditur);* true teaching is distinguished from false by a testing of spirits, rather than an official decree; there are references to sacraments, but no sense of sacramentalism; and the community, along with its interest in realized eschatology, still anticipates the Parousia.[63]

For these reasons Black can argue that the Johannine letters are not "fundamentally" documents of early Catholicism. Rather surprisingly, he also maintains that it would be possible to argue, on the basis of the same data, that these letters do show tendencies toward early Catholicism.[64] Although he does not undertake this analysis, he evidently wishes to make the point that even a carefully constructed, detailed definition of "early Catholicism" can point toward different results.

Black concludes by raising the question of whether the model of early Catholicism, as it is usually defined, is an adequate analytical tool. On the one hand, he suggests, it is anachronistic (using later rubrics such as "sacrament" and "orthodoxy"), but on the other, it employs sociological concepts (such as "tradition" and "hierarchical organization") that are not necessarily "Catholic" at all. The understanding of "early Catholicism," Black believes, must be sharpened if the concept is to be truly serviceable.[65]

The views of Brown, Kysar, and Black suggest that the components of "early Catholicism" may be more important than the term itself. Continuing research on the Johannine epistles should concern itself with the attitude toward tradition, the formulation of faith, the importance of ethics, the role of the sacraments, and other aspects of the life of the early church. The analysis of individual topics such as these may be more fruitful than an attempt to fit them into the definition of a broader rubric such as "early Catholicism."

The final section of this chapter describes some of the major characteristics and values that interpreters identify in the Johannine epistles. Some commentators, for example, highlight the prominence of Christian love in these writings. **Amos N. Wilder** maintains that "their appeal will continue to rest on the simplicity of their testimony that God is love and that love is the test of religion."[66]

George B. Caird notes that the commandment of love and belief in the incarnation are inseparably related. Christian love, he asserts, always recognizes its source in Jesus, the incarnate Son of God who displayed God's love in his ministry.[67]

From a very similar perspective, **Rudolf Bultmann** points out that the opponents of the author of 1 John fail to see that God's love for us is the basis of our love for God (4:10). As a consequence, they also fail to understand revelation as historical event.[68] Just as Caird relates Christian love to the incarnation, Bultmann

relates it to revelation in history. Although they use different terminology, both focus on Jesus as the one who revealed and exempli-
fied God's love for humanity.

Another accomplishment of the writer of 1 John is to balance
a "high" Christology with an appreciation of the earthly life of
Jesus. **Raymond E. Brown,** in particular, notes that the author and
his opponents both hold to the "high" Christology of pre-existence
and incarnation portrayed in the Gospel of John. In this respect they
share the same Johannine background. For the secessionists, this
Christology has the effect of negating the importance of the earthly
career of Jesus. The writer of 1 John adheres to the Johannine language of the pre-existence of Jesus, but he also affirms the salvific
importance of Jesus' earthly life.[69]

Robert Kysar identifies four areas in which he believes the
Johannine epistles have continuing value for Christians today.
Although he treats the letters together at this point, his comments
focus especially on 1 John. His summary may serve as an appropriate conclusion to this chapter on 1 John.

1) At the end of the first century, Kysar suggests, the church
recognized a need to define the difference between an authentic
Christian faith and an aberration of that faith. The first two letters of
John contributed two vital beliefs to this "emerging orthodoxy"—
the centrality of the humanity of Christ and the importance of the
moral dimension of Christian life.

2) Kysar notes further that 3 John illustrates the emergence of
a clear structure of authority in the church. Although the letter does
not specifically define that structure, it seeks to preserve good order
for the sake of the community.

3) The three Johannine epistles reflect a pastoral sensitivity
and mode of operation that have value today. The writers are aware
of the human condition and ways of nurturing people to deal with
that condition.

4) Kysar concludes that 1, 2, and 3 John, more than any other
writings in the New Testament, show how Christianity is rooted
and centered in love.[70]

5
2 John

The opening pages of the chapter on 1 John examined issues of authorship and date that arise in the study of all three Johannine letters. Readers may refer to those pages as they relate to 2 John. This chapter will begin with a discussion of "the elder" or "the presbyter" *(ho presbyteros),* who appears as the author of 2 John (v. 1) and 3 John (v. 1). The remainder of the chapter will focus on questions of occasion and setting, genre and structure, and major characteristics and concerns of 2 John.

The Elder

Attempts to identify the elder who wrote 2 and 3 John sometimes refer to the report from Papias, bishop of Hierapolis about 130–140 CE. According to Eusebius, Papias reported that he questioned anyone who had "attended the presbyters." Papias wanted to learn about the words of the "presbyters," but as examples of this group he mentions seven persons (Andrew, Peter, Philip, Thomas, James, John, and Matthew), whom he also calls "disciples of the Lord." He goes on to mention two others, a man named Aristion and the presbyter John, whom he also describes as disciples.[1]

As confusing as it is, this account does seem to indicate that Papias distinguished between two men named John—one a disciple (or apostle) and the other a presbyter (elder). It is not clear whether Papias regarded the "presbyters" as followers of the "disciples" or whether he thought of Aristion and the presbyter John as personal "disciples" of Jesus who were not among the twelve.[2]

If Papias spoke of "John the Elder" as a venerable figure in the early church and a distinct person from the apostle John, the question arises whether John the Elder wrote 2 and 3 John. **William Barclay** represents the view that this John was indeed the author of these letters.[3]

Amos N. Wilder, on the other hand, argues that the identity of John the Elder with the writer of the letters cannot simply be assumed.[4] In part, perhaps, because the account from Papias is so confusing, other recent commentators appear to be equally reluctant to focus on John the Elder in this connection. Most prefer to examine the meaning of "elder" with reference to Jewish and early Christian usage.

In Hellenistic Jewish usage, according to Wilder, the term "elder" could refer to an older person who was accorded a special office or dignity. In early Christianity, the term sometimes designated persons who held positions of leadership and authority in a local congregation. Wilder points out, however, that "the elder" who wrote 2 John is clearly assuming an authority that extends beyond the local church.[5]

Other writers agree that the term "elder" in 2 and 3 John does not simply designate an official in a local congregation. Like Wilder, Barclay points out that this elder assumes the right to speak to congregations other than his own.[6] **Rudolf Bultmann** suggests that the elder who wrote 3 John would not be a local official, since in that case he would give some indication of the church in which he held office.[7] **Rudolf Schnackenburg** points out that "the elder" or "the presbyter" never occurs in the singular for an individual member of the "presbyterium."[8]

If the elder who wrote 2 and 3 John has an authority extending beyond the local church, the question arises whether he holds an official position or simply enjoys an informal influence and prestige throughout the region. Recent commentators favor the latter alternative. **Raymond E. Brown** suggests that the status of the presbyter seems to be one "of prestige but not of juridical authority."[9]

Robert Kysar notes that the elder does not threaten any "official" action against the disobedient but employs persuasion and appeals to sound teaching. The elder is a revered leader of some sort, but this does not presuppose a position with official authority.[10] **Georg Strecker** suggests that the term "elder" seems to represent "a fixed title of honor," and he believes that the prestige of the elder led to the preservation of 2 and 3 John.[11]

A number of commentators emphasize the function of the elder in transmitting tradition from the apostolic period to later times. Wilder, for example, speaks of the elder as belonging to "those intermediate figures, between the apostles and the later leaders, who could vouch for the original apostolic witness."[12]

Similarly, Brown describes the elder as a "disciple of the disciples of Jesus and thus a second-generation figure" who transmitted tradition from the first generation. Further, Brown suggests, the elder might have been a disciple of the Beloved Disciple of the Gospel of John. This elder lived in a large Johannine community center and corresponded with smaller Johannine churches some distance away.[13]

With a similar emphasis on the Johannine community, Schnackenburg describes the elder as "an outstanding personality from the Johannine circle, perhaps an apostolic disciple, who represents the Johannine tradition and upholds it."[14]

Recent interpreters appear to have more confidence in describing the function of "the elder" of 2 and 3 John than in defining his position or identifying his name. The "traditional" view of authorship would find no difficulty on this point, for it holds that the apostle John wrote the Gospel of John and all three letters of John. Commentators who do not subscribe to the traditional view are more inclined to think of "the elder" as a second-generation figure who transmitted apostolic tradition to a later period.

Occasion and Setting

Amos N. Wilder provides a typical description of the occasion and setting of 2 John. He depicts it as a letter to a congregation, conveying the greeting of the elder and a sister church. The writer's emphasis on observing love and obeying the commandments suggests that false teaching about Jesus is associated with un-Christian practices (vv. 4–6).

The writer, Wilder continues, warns his readers against those who deny the coming of Jesus Christ "in the flesh" (v. 7; cf. 1 John 4:2). The author urges the recipients to not even greet "deceivers" who advocate false doctrine about Jesus, much less offer them hospitality (vv. 7–11). **William Barclay** and **Robert Kysar** provide similar descriptions.[15]

Noting that 2 John is addressed to "the elect lady and her children" (v. 1), Wilder suggests that this is a "gracious personification of a particular church" rather than a reference to a particular individual.[16] Barclay discusses the question whether the terms "elect" *(eklekte)* or "lady" *(kyria)* can be proper names. He concludes that it is possible, but highly improbable, that either word is a proper name. An argument he considers decisive is throughout the letter "the elect lady" is addressed sometimes in the singular (vv. 4, 5, 13) and sometimes in the plural (vv. 6, 8, 10, 12). Like many other commentators, Barclay concludes that the address must refer to a church.[17]

Some interpreters find a close connection between 1 John and 2 John. **Pheme Perkins,** for example, believes that the same person wrote both letters. She suggests that the author of 1 John may have composed 2 John as a "cover letter" that he directed to communities threatened by false teachers.[18]

Robert Kysar takes a similar position, even though he believes that one person wrote 1 John, and another wrote 2 and 3 John. He holds that 2 John seeks to protect individual churches from the threat presented by the same separatists who were criticized in 1 John.[19]

Genre and Structure

With regard to the genre of 2 John, **Rudolf Bultmann** seems to stand alone in his view that the letter form may be a fiction. He believes that the writer of 2 John utilized both 1 John and 3 John. The designation of the sender as "the elder" (v. 1) may imitate 3 John 1, and the conclusion (vv. 12–13) may imitate 3 John 13–14.[20]

Most interpreters regard 2 and 3 John as genuine letters. **Rudolf Schnackenburg** summarizes a number of major reasons for this. He points out that they are almost identical in length (1,126 and 1,105 characters, respectively), and they would each have filled a single sheet of papyrus. Their style (including certain phrases common in Hellenistic letter writing), the treatment of concrete issues, and the mention of specific individuals indicate that they were designed as real letters from the beginning.[21]

Robert Kysar calls attention to the elder's concern to establish a cordial relationship with his readers at the beginning of the letter and then remind them of this relationship at the conclusion. He offers the following outline of 2 John: salutation (vv. 1–2), apostolic greeting (v. 3), thanksgiving (v. 4), exhortations (vv. 5–11), closing (v. 12), greetings (v. 13).[22]

Rather surprisingly, in view of the letter's brevity, Schnackenburg gives a different outline: prescript (vv. 1–3), faithfulness to God's commandments (vv. 4–6), guarding against the heretical teachers (vv. 7–9), refusing hospitality to the heretics (vv. 10–11), intention to visit and final greetings (vv. 12–13).[23] As in the case of 1 John, specialists analyze the structure of the letter in different ways.

Major Characteristics and Concerns

Major characteristics and concerns of 2 John relate to the purpose of the letter, the phrase "teaching of Christ," and issues of orthodoxy and early Catholicism.

The question of the purpose of 2 John arises because the letter seems to fall into two disparate parts. In vv. 4–6, the writer advises his readers to show love to one another; in vv. 7–11, he urges them to have nothing to do with false teachers. The relation of these two parts remains a continuing problem for interpreters, since the attitude of Christian love is not reflected in the exclusionary attitude toward false teachers.

Rudolf Schnackenburg argues that the author's purpose is to oppose the heretical teachers who deny "the coming of Jesus Christ in the flesh" (v. 7 [RSV]). The author is afraid that even before he visits, some of these "deceivers" may come to the community and promote their teachings.[24] This view implies that the advice on practicing love (vv. 4–6) is ancillary to the warning against false teachers in the latter part of the letter (vv. 7–11). **Rudolf Bultmann** reflects the same viewpoint when he speaks of vv. 4–6 as preparing the way for vv. 7–11.[25]

Amos N. Wilder reverses this emphasis but then defines "love" in a broad sense that applies to both major sections of the letter (vv. 4–6 and 7–11). Commenting on v. 5—"I beg you…that we love one another" (RSV)—he states that this verse represents the whole purpose of the letter. He also argues that the love commandment is the sum of Christian instruction that differentiates Christians from the "deceivers" who have gone out into the "world" (v. 7).

In their "Docetic denial of Christ's humanity and passion," Wilder adds, these deceivers fail to understand "the full love of the Father and the true basis for our quickening fellowship with the Son."[26] In these ways Wilder articulates a comprehensive understanding of love that gives some unity to the two major parts of the letter.

An expression characteristic of 2 John is the phrase "teaching" or "doctrine" *(didache)* of Christ. The word "teaching" occurs three times in vv. 9–10. The first time, and possibly the second (depending on the Greek text that is read), it is followed by "of Christ." In any case, it seems clear that the "teaching of Christ," or "doctrine of Christ," is meant throughout these verses.

It is possible to understand the "teaching of Christ" as the early church's teaching with regard to Christ or the teaching that Christ himself gave. **Robert Kysar** understands it in the first sense, as the teaching or doctrine about Christ, with special reference to the belief in the genuine humanity of Jesus.[27] Wilder interprets the expression in a very similar way.[28]

Recently **C. Clifton Black** has suggested that both interpretations may be accurate. He indicates first that the writer probably meant the teaching about Christ—namely, his coming in the flesh. Black goes on to comment, "More so than modern interpreters, however, the elder would probably have equated, not distinguished, the church's proclamation about Jesus with Jesus' own (see 1 John 1:1–4)."[29] Black's reference to 1 John seems to imply that the writer of that letter regarded the church's tradition about Jesus as having its basis in the revelation that Jesus incarnated.

A final issue in the interpretation of 2 John concerns the evidence for any tendencies toward "early Catholicism." As in the case of 1 John, commentators show some reluctance to employ this expression. They do call attention, however, to developments in church organization or doctrine that could represent tendencies in this direction.

Rudolf Schnackenburg focuses on the writer's assumption that he can write to another congregation, give instructions for the treatment of heretical teachers, and state his intention to visit in person. Although the word "church" (*ekklesia*) does not occur in 2 John, Schnackenburg believes the letter reflects a church organization that "shows signs of the early stages of the development of monarchical episcopacy." This indicates, he suggests, that 2 John probably originated in Asia Minor, since the letters of Ignatius show that the monarchical episcopacy won acceptance very quickly in that area.[30]

In this connection **Robert Kysar** calls attention to the expression "teaching" or "doctrine of Christ" in 2 John. The fact that the humanity of Jesus has the status of "doctrine" contributes, he believes, to the emergence of an orthodoxy in the early church. This orthodoxy has its basis in the tradition represented in the Gospel of John (1:14), but at the same time it seeks to counter verses in the gospel that minimize Christ's human qualities (e.g., John 19:30).[31]

In a similar way, **Georg Strecker** argues that the concept of "teaching" in 2 John, while not explicitly opposed to "false doctrine," is closely associated with the term "truth." As such, he believes, it marks "the division between heresy and church." Strecker also notes, however, that this function of "teaching," or theological instruction, is as early as the letters of Paul. He also points out that the Johannine letters do not make an exclusive claim to truth on behalf of this teaching. Strecker's careful analysis of the concept of "teaching" reflects his emphasis on the difficulty of defining the expression "early Catholicism."[32]

6
3 John

With only 219 words in the Greek text, 3 John is the shortest writing in the New Testament.[1] The style may remind readers of the literary term "slice of life," since the letter provides an insight into a brief moment in a complex of relationships involving four early Christians, two delegations of itinerant preachers, and two or more congregations. The letter, unfortunately, does not explain how this situation developed or how it might be resolved. Interpreters must try to reconstruct, as well as they can, the occasion and setting, genre and structure, and major characteristics of 3 John.

Occasion and Setting

Amos N. Wilder provides a summary of the letter that introduces a number of critical issues. He notes that "the elder" writes to "the beloved Gaius," commending him for offering hospitality to traveling missionaries in the past and encouraging him to provide similar support for the present deputation (vv. 1–8). Then the elder criticizes a certain Diotrephes for not acknowledging his authority and not showing hospitality to visiting missionaries (vv. 9–10). In light of 1 and 2 John, Wilder thinks it likely that Diotrephes also belongs to the "deceivers" who promote false teaching about Jesus. Near the close, the elder commends a person named Demetrius, perhaps the bearer of the letter (v. 12).[2]

This summary touches on the question whether 1, 2, and 3 John all refer to the same situation. The first two letters are closely related because both speak of false teachers who deny that Jesus Christ came "in the flesh" (1 John 4:2; 2 John 7). The second and third letters are closely related by virtue, presumably, of common authorship by "the elder" (2 John 1; 3 John 1). If these connections are sufficiently close to justify the belief that all the letters address the same situation, then it is possible to interpret 3 John in relation to 1 and 2 John. As it was noted above, Wilder follows this procedure in arguing that Diotrephes was probably one of the false teachers with divergent views of Jesus.

The author of 3 John is gracious and generous in his praise of Gaius, the addressee. **Rudolf Schnackenburg** describes Gaius as "a friendly member of the laity."[3] **William Barclay,** more critically, comments that Gaius "represents the good, well-meaning man" who cannot decide what to do. Barclay admits, however, that the outcome of the situation is not known.[4] On the basis of 3 John 4, in which the elder mentions "my children," some commentators suggest that the elder had perhaps converted Gaius to Christianity.[5]

Interpreters differ on the question whether Gaius and Diotrephes belong to the same congregation. Wilder believes that they do not. If they did, he argues, Gaius would not be ignorant of the details mentioned in vv. 9–10.[6] Other commentators suggest that Gaius and Diotrephes may belong to the same church.[7] These commentators do not address, however, the argument that Wilder makes.

The elder depicts Diotrephes negatively, as someone who "likes to put himself first" and rejects the elder's authority (v. 9). Schnackenburg notes that in the following verse the elder makes four additional criticisms of Diotrephes—he spreads false charges against the elder, regarding missionary policy and perhaps other issues; he refuses to show hospitality to the missionaries; he prevents other members of the community from showing such hospitality (Gaius was one of these, but in his case, at least, the attempt was unsuccessful); he tries to expel his opponents from the church (again, in the case of Gaius, this attempt was evidently unsuccessful).[8]

Diotrephes appears to be an ambitious person who wants to exercise authority. As Black remarks, the elder accuses him of a "hunger for power."[9] It is not clear, however, exactly how he seeks to "put himself first." Wilder believes that Diotrephes may oppose the elder because he wants to assume power, as an individual leader, in one of the "household churches" of the area.[10] Barclay, focusing on the different types of church leadership, thinks that Diotrephes represents the settled ministry of elders in local congregations, who regard itinerant preachers as intruders.[11]

Pheme Perkins finds no evidence that Diotrephes seeks to establish a monarchic episcopate of the kind mentioned in the letters of Ignatius of Antioch, even though he wants to enjoy the same authority in his church that the elder has in his own.[12] From a somewhat different point of view, Schnackenburg argues that Diotrephes, as the sole leader of the community, represents a period of transition in which the monarchical episcopate is "in the process of being established."[13]

Interpreters also differ on the question whether Diotrephes seeks to promote divergent theological views. The author of 3 John does not explicitly claim that this is so. His criticisms of Diotrephes refer to practical matters of congregational authority and organization (vv. 9–10) rather than theological convictions. In a similar way, some modern commentators—for example, **Pheme Perkins** and **Rudolf Bultmann**—limit the role of Diotrephes to issues of authority and organization.[14]

Amos N. Wilder does argue that Diotrephes is causing problems in the area of Christian beliefs as well as church organization. Reading 3 John in light of 1 and 2 John, Wilder considers it likely that Diotrephes belongs to the "deceivers" who promote false teaching about Jesus. These theological differences, Wilder suggests, may be even more important than Diotrephes' assertion of local autonomy and individual leadership.[15]

Approaching this issue from a different point of view, **C. Clifton Black** argues that Diotrephes could well be concerned about protecting doctrinal standards. He suggests that Diotrephes may refuse to accept missionary delegations out of the fear that "his community's doctrinal standards might be contaminated."[16] Whereas Wilder associates Diotrephes with the false teachers of 1 and 2 John, Black thinks it possible that he actually opposes those who promote false teachings.

Robert Kysar also presents a sympathetic view of Diotrephes, arguing that he is not a separatist like those in 1 and 2 John. On the contrary, he tries to preserve his own community by making it independent of the parent body and refusing to receive representatives from either side of the schism. The elder fears that the group to which Gaius and Diotrephes belong may drift away from the parent body, and he writes to enlist Gaius' help in preventing this occurrence.[17]

It is clear that scholars differ in reconstructing the role of Diotrephes. Some limit his role to matters of authority and organization in the church, while others extend it to issues of doctrine. In the latter instance, some understand Diotrephes as one of the "deceivers," and others see him as a guardian of correct doctrine. One factor here is that some scholars interpret more "contextually" than others. Some would argue that the larger context justifies a theological role for Diotrephes, while others would limit their reconstruction to the explicit statements in 3 John 9–10.

The elder mentions Demetrius in v. 12, indicating that he "has testimony" from three sources—from "everyone," from "the truth itself," and from the elder. **Rudolf Schnackenburg** suggests three possible roles for Demetrius: he may be one of the itinerant preachers referred to in vv. 3–8; he may be one of their leaders; he may also be the bearer of the present letter.[18] As a fourth possibility, **Georg Strecker** suggests that Demetrius may be the "middleman" between the elder and the community of Diotrephes. In this role, he is to receive special support from Gaius.[19]

Similarly, Black argues that Demetrius, by implication, is the elder's envoy to the church with which Gaius is associated. Black believes that 3 John is specifically a letter of introduction and recommendation, and its "clearest motive" is to commend Demetrius in his role as envoy.[20] This interesting interpretation emphasizes the importance of Demetrius himself, so that he becomes, in effect, the principal figure in the letter rather than someone mentioned incidentally toward the end.

Genre and Structure

As in the case of 1 and 2 John, it is interesting that specialists differ in providing outlines for 3 John. The variations in this instance reflect individual approaches to the letter. **Robert Kysar** gives an outline based on typical components of the ancient epistolary form. **Rudolf Schnackenburg** divides the letter into sections dealing with Gaius, Diotrephes, and Demetrius—the three persons mentioned by name. **C. Clifton Black** provides an outline following the form of the ancient letter of introduction and recommendation.

Kysar emphasizes that the elder, as in 2 John, first establishes a cordial relationship with the readers, then provides "epistolary exhortation," and closes on the note of personal relationship with which the letter began. The form that 3 John follows consists of salutation (v. 1), prayer (v. 2), thanksgiving (v. 3), exhortations (vv. 5–11), commendation (v. 12), closing (vv. 13–14), and peace and greetings (v. 15).[21]

Schnackenburg outlines the letter with reference to the three principal figures: prescript (v. 1), praise for Gaius and a request to support itinerant preachers (vv. 2–8), the behavior of Diotrephes (vv. 9–10), commendation of Demetrius (vv. 11–12), and conclusion (vv. 13–15).[22]

Black believes that 3 John follows the form of the ancient letter of recommendation, although it deviates slightly by postponing to the end the identification of Demetrius as the principal subject. He gives the following outline: opening (saluting Gaius, v. 1; praying for health, rejoicing in truth, vv. 2–4), body (supporting missionaries, vv. 5–8; condemning Diotrephes, vv. 9–10; commending Demetrius (vv. 11–12), closing (regrets, hopes, and greetings, vv. 13–15).[23]

Major Characteristics and Concerns

Several interpreters call attention to features of special importance in 3 John. **Robert Kysar** and **Georg Strecker** touch on the question of "early Catholicism," without trying to emphasize the phrase itself. **C. Clifton Black** notes especially the language of "family" in 3 John as a metaphor for the church.

Kysar observes that 3 John reflects a situation in which an "unofficial organizational structure" has emerged in the Johannine community. As a result, the terms "church" (vv. 6, 9–10) and "elder" (v. 1) have come into use.[24] To this limited extent, Kysar seems willing to recognize a process of organizational development.

Strecker notes that 3 John 10 is sometimes understood to mean that the communities behind the Johannine letters live "under an episcopal constitution that includes canon law and a praxis of excommunication." Strecker argues, however, that an analogy to Diotrephes' action in excluding church members is reported also for Paul (1 Cor 5:1–5; 2 Cor 2:6; 7:11). He also observes that there is no evidence in 3 John that Diotrephes exercised an authority "legalized by the principle of succession."[25]

Noting the use of terms such as "brothers," "friends," and "children," Black calls attention to the language of family as a metaphor for the church in 3 John. In contrast to the Roman concept of "paternal authority" *(patria potestas),* which gave the father extensive dominion over the household, Black suggests that the author of 3 John depicts "an essentially egalitarian Johannine community."[26]

To a limited extent, Kysar and Strecker recognize the presence of hierarchical organization and authoritarian relationships in the church or churches *influenced* by Diotrephes. Black believes that the elder himself—even though he enjoys the status of "elder"—prefers to think in terms of horizontal, egalitarian relationships within the church community. If data were available, it would be rewarding to explore the question of how the elder balances his sense of authority with the egalitarian understanding of the church that his language seems to imply.

7
Jude

Readers may wish to read the chapter on 2 Peter and the present chapter in close conjunction with each other, since most of the material in Jude has parallels in 2 Peter. The treatment of 2 Peter discussed theories that seek to explain the literary relationship between the two letters. As much as possible, this chapter will focus on Jude itself, dealing with issues of authorship and date, sources and affinities, occasion and setting, genre and structure, and major characteristics and concerns.

Authorship and Date

The letter of Jude identifies its author as "Jude [Judas], a servant of Jesus Christ and brother of James" (1:1). Interpreters explain this verse in two different ways. Some support the "traditional" view that finds a reference to the Jude and James mentioned in the gospels as brothers of Jesus (Matt 13:55; Mark 6:3). Other commentators attribute the letter to a later author who wrote in the name and spirit of Jude, the brother of Jesus and James. The first theory allows for an early date for the letter— sometime during the apostolic period—while the second view implies a later date.

A number of scholars support the traditional view of authorship. **Thomas W. Leahy,** for example, believes that the author is "almost certainly" the Jude mentioned among the "brothers of the Lord" in Mark 6:3. The reference to "the predictions of the apostles" (v. 17), he argues, does not have to mean that the author is looking back to the apostles as figures of an earlier time. It can signify only that he does not include himself among them—that is, he is not the apostle Jude mentioned in Luke 6:16 and Acts 1:13.[1]

Leahy also approaches the question of authorship from the standpoint of the relation between 2 Peter and Jude. If 2 Peter uses Jude as a source, as he believes, then one must be cautious about assigning too late a date to Jude. One must think in terms of a relatively early date, and this in turn supports the theory of authorship by Jude the brother of Jesus.[2]

Norman Hillyer argues that nothing in the letter requires a date beyond the lifetime of Jude the brother of Jesus. The references to the Parousia (vv. 1, 14, 21, 24) reflect the expectations of the first century rather than the second. The antinomian heresy that Jude attacks was also widespread in the first century, even though it became more prevalent in the second.[3]

In a similar way, **Richard Bauckham** holds that it is not necessary to posit a late date for Jude. Since "early Catholicism" is not applicable to this letter, and the opponents are not advocating Gnosticism, a late date is not required. Although Jude speaks of "the faith" in the objective sense of "what is believed" (v. 3), this does not necessarily designate a fixed body of doctrine. It can refer simply to the gospel, as in Gal 1:23. The reference to the apostles (v. 17) does not have to mean that the author is looking back on the apostolic age as a period in the past. It can refer to the prophecy or teaching that the apostles gave when they founded churches.

Bauckham concludes that a date in the 50s is very plausible, indicating that Jude might be one of the earliest New Testament writings. The author could well have been Jude the brother of Jesus. This Jude, Bauckham adds, could have acquired the competence in Greek that the letter displays.[4]

Interpreters who regard Jude as a later, pseudonymous writing address many of the same issues—for example, the nature of "the faith," the reference to "the apostles," and the views of the opponents—but they interpret them differently.

Albert E. Barnett, for example, argues that the author of the letter could hardly be Jude the brother of Jesus and James. The author, he believes, understands faith in essentially creedal terms, venerates the apostles as figures of the past, and regards his opponents as Docetists or Gnostics. These factors indicate that an unknown author wrote Jude about 115 CE.[5]

Many other scholars also believe that "the faith…once for all delivered to the saints" (v. 3 [RSV]) must refer to a deposit of tradition received from the apostolic period. Many think that the author, in referring to "the predictions of the apostles" (v. 17), is looking back on them as figures of the past. Some interpreters believe that the author regards his opponents as Docetists or Gnostics, rather than simply antinomians. Those who echo one or more of these arguments include **J. Christiaan Beker, Thomas W. Leahy, Claude H. Thompson, Jerome H. Neyrey, Pheme Perkins,** and **Pierre Reymond.**[6]

John H. Elliott and **Jerome H. Neyrey** also call attention to other arguments which, they believe, support a later date for Jude. Elliott emphasizes the letter's literary style and vocabulary, which suggest that the author is a Hellenistic Jewish Christian. He believes that the author opposes troublemakers who resemble Gnostic heretics. The author writes in Jude's name, with stress on his relation to James, within a circle of early Christians most likely in Syria or northern Palestine perhaps in the period 70–100 CE.[7]

Reflecting his interest in insights from the social sciences, Neyrey seeks to establish the "social location" of the author of Jude. He is, Neyrey believes, a second-generation member of the group who does not consider himself to be an apostle (vv. 3, 17). He exhibits a scribal background—he can write letters, uses good Greek, shows a fine rhetorical style, refers to esoteric Jewish writings (*Testament of Moses,* v. 9; 1 *Enoch,* vv. 14–15), and shows a knowledge of Jewish lore and traditions. He has, presumably, a non-elite status as a member of an urban retainer class.[8]

Throughout the period covered by this book, there does not appear to be any trend in favor of either theory of authorship, the "traditional" or the "anonymous." Specialists have advocated both theories, and in this sense the question invites further study and discussion.

Sources and Affinities

The discussion of sources in Chapter 3 indicated that most scholars believe 2 Peter used Jude as a source, rather than vice versa. Apart from this question, **Richard J. Bauckham** lists a number of sources that, he holds, Jude utilizes.

These include the Old Testament, in its Hebrew text rather than the Septuagint; the Jewish apocryphal writings *Testament of Moses* and *1 Enoch;* Jewish paraenetic and haggadic traditions, which cannot be related to any particular written source; Christian traditions, consisting of catechetical (vv. 20–23) and liturgical (vv. 24–25) material; the writer's own summary of early Christian missionary teaching (v. 18); and possibly a quotation from a Christian prophetic oracle (v. 11).[9]

Occasion and Setting

The category of "Occasion and Setting" deals with issues such as the place of origin of Jude, its destination, and the identity of the opponents or troublemakers who "secretly slipped in" among the recipients (v. 4 [author's translation]). The letter provides few clues for answering these questions. Commentators must rely on educated guesses, if indeed they try to provide answers at all.

Albert E. Barnett suggests that the use of Jude by 2 Peter, which was probably written in Rome, may indicate that Jude also originated in Rome. The acknowledgment of Jude as canonical by Tertullian and the Muratorian Fragment also points to Rome. The letter's severe condemnation of heresy, its polemical character, and its high regard for authority may also reflect an origin in Rome.

Barnett regards the letter as encyclical in nature, intended for Christendom in general, although he also suggests that it might be addressed especially to the churches in Asia Minor. Its message, he believes, is intended for Christians wherever unity is endangered by the heretical teaching and immoral practices of Docetism.[10]

Bo Reicke groups Jude together with James, 2 Peter, and *1 Clement*. He believes that all four were probably written in the 90s, and all four emphasize the importance of a cooperative attitude to the Roman state as an essential condition for the success of the gospel. Although he notes that *1 Clement* was written from Rome, he does not specifically propose that Jude had the same origin. Reicke does note that Jude contains some Old Testament references that do not occur in 2 Peter, and he suggests that it may be directed more to Jewish Christians.[11]

Other writers support this view that Jude may be addressed especially to Jewish Christians. **Thomas W. Leahy** believes that Jude is addressed to communities threatened by false teaching, which may be "an embryonic form of antinomian Christian Gnosticism." These communities may consist of Jewish Christians in the Diaspora, possibly in Syria.[12]

Richard J. Bauckham also thinks that the letter is addressed to a predominantly Jewish-Christian community. Because the opponents are antinomians, he suggests further that this community is located in a Gentile environment.[13] Bauckham believes that Asia Minor is a more probable destination than Syria, because Syria was the one area of the later church that did not accept Jude as canonical.[14]

Duane F. Watson outlines several possibilities. If the author is Jude the brother of Jesus, then he is probably writing to a church in Palestine. If someone else wrote the letter in Jude's name, then he could be sending it to a church in Asia Minor, which contained large Jewish populations in a Gentile environment. Finally, Watson suggests, the writer could have sent the letter to Egypt, where it later became popular with Clement of Alexandria and Origen.[15]

If scholars reach no consensus about the provenance or destination of Jude, they also have different theories about the identity of the false teachers who are causing so much trouble among the recipients of the letter (v. 4). Some interpreters regard these persons as antinomians who engage in immoral and divisive behavior (vv. 4, 8, 10–13, 16, 19). Others argue that the false teachers are not only antinomians, but also Gnostics or Docetists of some kind.

Among recent commentators, **Richard J. Bauckham** and **Duane F. Watson** represent the view that the false teachers are antinomians only. Bauckham believes, for example, that they are evidently itinerant charismatics who have come to the church or churches to which Jude is writing. There is no "secure exegetical evidence" that they promulgate Gnostic teachings. They are, Bauckham asserts, libertines or antinomians *in principle,* rather than Gnostics who advocate immoral behavior.[16] The missing element in their teaching, he notes, is "the cosmological dualism of true Gnosticism."[17]

Bauckham illustrates this interpretation by referring to certain key verses in Jude. The false teachers, he argues, evidently understand the grace of God in Christ (v. 4) to mean deliverance from all moral restraint. Their denial of Christ (v. 4) does not involve doctrinal error, but signifies a rejection of his moral demands. Their disparagement of angels (vv. 8–10) involves a rejection of the angels' role as guardians of the law and the moral order of the world.[18]

Similarly, Watson sees the opponents of Jude as antinomians but evidently not as Gnostics. These people revile the angels who guard the law of Moses (vv. 8–10), but they are not thinking in terms of a cosmic dualism in which angels have the role of demigods of the material universe. Their indulgence in sin does not result from a dualistic emphasis on "spirit" and "knowledge" in contrast to the material body.[19]

Other interpreters understand the false teachers as antinomians and also Gnostics or Docetists. **Albert E. Barnett,** for example, argues that to deny Jesus (v. 4) is to deny Christian teaching about Jesus, and therefore to accept both Docetism and licentiousness. As Docetists, the false teachers reject authority (v. 8), holding the angels in contempt because angels were involved in creating the material world.[20]

J. Christiaan Beker speaks of the false teachers as early Gnostics of some kind. As such, he believes, they claim special visions (v. 8), regard themselves as spiritual men elevated in a spiritual realm (vv. 8, 12, 15), and promote divisions in the church (v. 19).[21] **William Barclay** calls attention to the word "only," used of Christ (v. 4) and of God (v. 25). Jude uses the word, he believes, because Gnostic opponents question the uniqueness of Christ and God.[22]

Barclay and **Pierre Reymond** both find a reflection of Gnostic anthropology in v. 19. The Gnostics divided human beings into ordinary people (animated by *psyche,* the principle of physical life) and spiritual people (endowed with *pneuma,* the highly developed spirit enabling them to have knowledge and experience of God). Although the false teachers claim to be "spiritual people" or "pneumatics," they are in fact "devoid of the Spirit" and are "ordinary people" or "psychics" (v. 19 [author's translation]). This distinction between two classes of people appears in some Gnostic movements, and Paul also refers to it (1 Cor 2:11–16).[23]

The question whether Jude is opposing antinomians only, or Gnostics and Docetists as well, remains a topic for continuing investigation. Beker, Barclay, and Reymond, for example, call attention to certain verses that they understand as directed against Gnostics. The exegetical problem is to determine whether these verses can be explained adequately in terms of opposition to antinomians alone.

Genre and Structure

With regard to the genre of Jude, commentators would appear to be unanimous in assuming that it is indeed a letter. Many do not raise the questions of what kind of letter it is or what structural elements it contains. Recently, however, **Richard J. Bauckham, Norman Hillyer,** and **Duane F. Watson** have addressed these issues, calling attention to features of Jude that may well facilitate a richer understanding on the part of readers.

Bauckham regards Jude as a genuine letter, sent to specific addressees and dealing with a specific situation. At the same time, he suggests that the body of the letter is more like a homily, consisting of a midrash on certain scriptural passages (vv. 5–19) and a paraenetic section or appeal (vv. 20–23). For this reason he describes Jude as an "epistolary sermon."[24]

Bauckham labels the exegetical section (vv. 5–19) as "A Midrash on Four Prophecies of the Doom of the Ungodly." Like the Qumran commentaries and much early Christian exegesis, this section reflects the hermeneutical assumptions that scripture is prophetic of the last time, and the writer and his readers are living in this time. This midrash, however, is not the main part of the letter. The climax comes in the appeal (vv. 20–23), which explains what "contending for the faith" involves and represents Jude's main purpose in writing.[25]

Bauckham also finds a careful chiastic structure in Jude. The letter begins, he notes, with an address and greeting (vv. 1–2) and ends with a concluding doxology (vv. 24–25). The exhortation to contend for the faith (v. 3) is explained by the paraenesis and positive Christian teaching at the close of the main body of the letter (vv. 20–23). The warning against false teachers (v. 4) is supported by the midrash arguing that these false teachers are the ungodly people of the last days predicted in scripture (vv. 5–19).[26] This chiasmus has the form, therefore, of ABCC'B'A'.

Hillyer and Watson call attention to triple expressions as a noteworthy stylistic device of Jude that is not characteristic of

2 Peter. Hillyer mentions "called loved, kept" (v. 1), "mercy, peace, love" (v. 2), and "Cain, Balaam, Korah" (v. 11). As further examples, Watson adds the references to the people from Egypt, the angels that left their proper dwelling, and Sodom and Gomorrah and the surrounding cities (vv. 5–7). He also notes the series of verbs "defile, reject, revile" (v. 8). For a document as short as it is, Jude seems to have an unexpectedly large number of these triplets.[27]

Watson also characterizes Jude in terms of the rhetorical conventions that, he believes, Jude the brother of Jesus had the opportunity to learn as he grew up in Galilee. He understands the letter primarily as an example of deliberative rhetoric, which seeks to persuade an audience to accept "what is advantageous, necessary, and expedient." The letter also utilizes epideictic rhetoric, which undertakes to "uplift what is honorable and cast down what is dishonorable…"[28]

From a different point of view, Watson divides Jude into major rhetorical categories of the time. The *exordium* (v. 3) seeks to gain the attention of the audience and introduce the reasons for writing. The *narratio* (v. 4) states the main points to be developed. The *probatio* (vv. 5–16) presents proofs to substantiate the propositions of the *narratio*. The *peroratio* summarizes the main points and appeals for the approval of the audience.[29] As in the case of Bauckham's analysis of Jude as an extended chiasmus, it is interesting that so short a letter can illustrate these rhetorical categories.

Major Characteristics and Concerns

Characteristics and concerns of Jude include the meaning of "faith" in v. 3, the question of "early Catholicism," and the relevance of this letter for today.

Interpreters of the New Testament often make a distinction between two types of faith, *fides quae creditur* and *fides qua creditur.* The first type is objective, signifying a fixed body of doctrine that is believed. The second calls attention to the subjective response of the individual believer. It is, in **Thomas W. Leahy's** words, "the response of total commitment to God's salvific revelation."[30] In interpreting any particular occurrence of the word "faith" in the New Testament, exegetes must ask which type the writer may have had in mind.

The writer of Jude appeals to his readers to "contend for the faith which was once for all delivered to the saints" (v. 3 [RSV]). Many commentators understand this verse as a reference to a "deposit of faith," a fixed body of doctrines accepted as orthodox and transmitted from the apostolic period to a later generation. This understanding of the verse supports the view that a later author wrote the letter in the name of Jude the brother of James and Jesus.

As noted above, **Richard J. Bauckham** and **Duane F. Watson** believe that "faith" in v. 3 refers simply to the gospel rather than a developed body of doctrines. The significance of their argument is that it introduces a distinction between two types of *fides quae creditur.* This distinction, in turn, affects the understanding of authorship and date. If "faith" in v. 3 signifies the gospel, then the possibility remains open that Jude the brother of Jesus wrote the letter, perhaps around the middle of the first century.

Bauckham and Watson also argue that the concept of "early Catholicism" is not applicable to the letter of Jude. They both focus on three developments that are usually considered characteristic of this phenomenon: the understanding of faith as a fixed body of beliefs, the waning of eschatological expectation, and the growth of institutional offices in the church.

Both scholars argue that "faith" in vv. 3 and 20 refers simply to the gospel, as it does in Gal 1:23. The idea of a body of orthodox doctrines does not need to be read into Jude's use of "faith," any more than it does into Paul's. Both argue that Jude maintains a vivid hope for the Parousia of the Lord (vv. 1, 14, 21, 24). They also stress that Jude appeals to the whole church, rather than ecclesiastical officials, to deal with the problems caused by the false teachers.[31]

Many commentators recognize that modern readers may have difficulty understanding Jude's idiom and applying its message today. Perhaps as clearly as anyone, **Albert E. Barnett** paraphrases Jude's advice to his readers for living as Christians (vv. 17–23): Jude counsels them to remember the predictions of the apostles, build themselves up on the foundation of their faith, pray in the Holy Spirit, remain in the love of God, wait for the coming of Jesus Christ and the gift of eternal life, and maintain a redemptive interest in those who are confused by heretical teaching.[32]

Notes

Introduction

    1. Robert L. Webb, "Epistles, Catholic," ABD vol. 2, ed. David Noel Freedman et al. (New York: Doubleday, 1992), 569–70.

    2. Ibid.

    3. Ibid.

    4. Raymond E. Brown, *The Epistles of John,* AB vol. 30 (Garden City, NY: Doubleday, 1982), 3–4.

    5. Ibid., 4.

    6. Ibid., 5.

    7. Pheme Perkins, *First and Second Peter, James, and Jude* (Louisville, KY: John Knox Press, 1995), 1.

    8. Ibid., 1–2.

1. James

    1. Franz Mussner, *Der Jakobusbrief,* HTKNT 13 (Freiburg: Herder, 1964), 18, 21.

    2. Ibid., 18–19.

    3. Ibid., 19–21.

    4. Ibid., 21–22.

    5. George Eldon Ladd, *A Theology of the New Testament* (Grand Rapids, MI: William B. Eerdmans, 1974), 589.

    6. Ibid., 589–600.

    7. Peter H. Davids, *The Epistle of James,* NIGTC (Exeter: Paternoster Press, 1982), 13.

    8. Ibid., 22.

9. Cain Hope Felder, "James," in *The International Bible Commentary,* ed. William R. Farmer et al., 1786–1801 (Collegeville, MN: Liturgical Press, 1998), 1787.

10. Luke Timothy Johnson, *The Letter of James,* AB vol. 37A (New York: Doubleday, 1995), 182–83; quotation 182.

11. Douglas J. Moo, *The Letter of James,* PNTC (Grand Rapids, MI/Cambridge, UK: William B. Eerdmans, 2000), 9–11, 15–18, 31.

12. Burton Scott Easton, "The Epistle of James," in IB 12, 1–74 (New York and Nashville: Abingdon Press, 1957), 6–9.

13. Arnold Meyer, *Das Raetsel des Jacobusbriefes,* BZNW 10 (Giessen: Alfred Toepelmann, 1930), 176–77, 300–307.

14. Ibid., 167.

15. Ibid., 167, 298.

16. Easton, "The Epistle of James," 10.

17. Ibid., 9–11, 14–15.

18. Albert E. Barnett, "James, Letter of," in IDB vol. E-J, ed. George A. Buttrick et al., 794–99 (New York and Nashville: Abingdon Press, 1962), 795.

19. Bo Reicke, *The Epistles of James, Peter, and Jude,* AB vol. 37 (Garden City, NY: Doubleday, 1964), xxi–xxiv.

20. Ibid., 4–6, 12.

21. Richard L. Scheef Jr., "The Letter of James," in IOVCB, ed. Charles M. Laymon, 916–923 (Nashville and New York: Abingdon Press, 1971), 916–17.

22. Martin Dibelius, *James: A Commentary on the Epistle of James,* rev. H. Greeven, trans. M. A. Williams. Hermeneia (Philadelphia: Fortress, 1976), 17–18, 47.

23. R. A. Martin, *James,* in R. A. Martin and John H. Elliott, *James/I–II Peter/Jude,* ACNT (Minneapolis, MN: Augsburg, 1982), 11–12, 19; quotation 12.

24. Sophie Laws, "James, Epistle of," in ABD vol. 3, 621–628, ed. David Noel Freedman et al. (New York: Doubleday, 1992), 622, 624; quotation 622.

25. Pheme Perkins, *First and Second Peter, James, and Jude.* (Louisville, KY: John Knox Press, 1995), 83–85.

26. Easton, "The Epistle of James," 4–5, 9–14.

27. Jean Cantinat, *Les Epitres de Saint Jacques et de Saint Jude* (Paris: Librairie Lecoffre, J. Gabalda et Cie., 1973), 15.

28. Laws, "James, Epistle of," 623.

29. Mussner, *Der Jakobusbrief,* 80, 83–84; quotation 80.

30. Johnson, *The Letter of James,* 79.

31. Moo, *The Letter of James,* 8, 33–34.

32. Easton, "The Epistle of James," 6.

33. Laws, "James, Epistle of," 624–625.

34. Cantinat, *Les Epitres de Saint Jacques et de Saint Jude,* 27. Cantinat gives a full page of parallels between James and Matthew and occasionally James and Luke, 27–28.

35. Mussner, *Der Jakobusbrief,* 52–53.

36. Dibelius, *James,* 28–29; Davids, *The Epistle of James,* 16; Laws, "James, Epistle of," 625; Johnson, *The Letter of James,* 180–181.

37. Reicke, *The Epistles of James, Peter, and Jude,* 18, 21–23.

38. Thomas W. Leahy, "The Epistle of James," in JBC, ed. Raymond E. Brown, Joseph A. Fitzmyer, and Roland E. Murphy, 369–377 (Englewood Cliffs, NJ: Prentice-Hall, 1968), 371.

39. Laws, "James, Epistle of," 624.

40. Davids, *The Epistle of James,* 18, 28–34.

41. Mussner, *Der Jakobusbrief,* 11, 61–62.

42. Moo, *The Letter of James,* 9–11.

43. Felder, "James," 1787.

44. Laws, "James, Epistle of," 624.

45. Easton, "The Epistle of James," 15–16.

46. Mussner, *Der Jakobusbrief,* 22.

47. Perkins, *First and Second Peter, James, and Jude,* 95; Barnett, "James, Letter of," 795–797; Cantinat, *Les Epitres de Saint Jacques et de Saint Jude,* 53–54.

48. Leahy, "The Epistle of James," 376; Davids, *The Epistle of James,* 14 and 14nn45–46; Laws, "James, Epistle of," 623.

49. Easton, "The Epistle of James," 35–39; Davids, *The Epistle of James,* 18; Johnson, *The Letter of James,* 182; Reicke, *The Epistles of James, Peter, and Jude,* 6.

50. Laws, "James, Epistle of," 623.

51. Dibelius, *James,* 1, 3, 5–11; quotation 3.

52. Easton, "The Epistle of James," 3–4; quotation 4.

53. Mussner, *Der Jakobusbrief,* 23–24; quotation 24; Cantinat, *Les Epitres de Saint Jacques et de Saint Jude,* 15–16.

54. Barnett, "James, Letter of," 795–796.

55. Leo G. Perdue, "Parenesis and the Epistle of James," ZNW 72 (1981): 250–255; quotation 250–251.

56. Thomas W. Leahy, "James, Epistle of St.," in NCE vol. 7, 816–817 (New York: McGraw-Hill: 1967), 817.

57. Davids, *The Epistle of James,* 13, 24–25.

58. Felder, "James," 1798.

59. Johnson, *The Letter of James,* 178–179; quotation 178.

60. Moo, *The Letter of James,* 8–9, 46.

61. Laws, "James, Epistle of," 621–622; Johnson, *The Letter of James,* 177.

62. Ladd, *A Theology of the New Testament,* 593.

63. Davids, *The Epistle of James,* 131.

64. Leahy, "The Epistle of James," 373; cf. Moo, *The Letter of James,* 126.

65. Martin, *James,* 28–31.

66. Easton, "The Epistle of James," 9–10, 41; cf. Scheef, "The Letter of James," 919–920; Cantinat, *Les Epitres de Saint Jacques et de Saint Jude,* 42–43.

67. Ladd, *A Theology of the New Testament,* 592–593; cf. Laws, "James, Epistle of," 625.

68. Adolf Schlatter, *Der Brief des Jakobus,* 2nd ed. (Stuttgart: Calwer Verlag, 1956), 187.

69. Davids, *The Epistle of James,* 50.

70. Mussner, *Der Jakobusbrief,* 22.

71. Davids, *The Epistle of James,* 119.

72. Martin, *James,* 31.

73. Dan O. Via Jr., "The Right Strawy Epistle Reconsidered: A Study in Biblical Ethics and Hermeneutics," JR 49 (1969): 257, 267.

74. Johnson, *The Letter of James,* 179–180.

75. Mussner, *Der Jakobusbrief,* 5th ed. 1987, 254–258; quotations 254–255.

76. William R. Baker, *Personal Speech-Ethics in the Epistle of James,* WUNT 2.68 (Tübingen: J. C. B. Mohr [Paul Siebeck], 1995), 2–3, 98–104, 287; quotation 2.

77. E. P. Sanders, *Paul and Palestinian Judaism: A Comparison of Patterns of Religion* (Philadelphia: Fortress Press, 1977), 420, 433, 426–427.

78. Moo, *The Letter of James,* 39–40, 42; quotation 40.

2. 1 Peter

1. Archibald M. Hunter, "The First Epistle of Peter," IB vol. 12, 75–159 (New York and Nashville: Abingdon Press, 1957), 78.

2. Ibid., 78–80, 144–145, 157–158.

3. Ibid., 80.

4. Edward G. Selwyn, *The First Epistle of St. Peter* (London: Macmillan, 1961), 32, 56–60; quotation 32.

5. W. C. van Unnik, "Peter, First Letter of," IDB vol. K-Q, ed. George A. Buttrick et al., 758–766 (New York and Nashville: Abingdon Press, 1962), 764–765.

6. Bo Reicke, *The Epistles of James, Peter, and Jude,* AB vol. 37 (Garden City, NY: Doubleday, 1964), 70–71, 133; Joseph A. Fitzmyer, "The First Epistle of Peter," JBC, ed. Raymond E. Brown, Joseph A. Fitzmyer, and Roland E. Murphy, 362–368 (Englewood Cliffs, NJ: Prentice-Hall, 1968), 362.

7. Norman Hillyer, *1 and 2 Peter, Jude,* NIBC (Peabody, MA: Hendrickson Publishers, 1992), 9.

8. Leonhard Goppelt, *A Commentary on 1 Peter,* ed. Ferdinand Hahn, trans. John E. Alsup (Grand Rapids, MI: William B. Eerdmans, 1993), 45–47.

9. David L. Bartlett, "The First Letter of Peter," NIB vol. 12, 227–319 (Nashville: Abingdon Press, 1998), 230, 234–235, 251.

10. John H. Elliott, *A Home for the Homeless: A Sociological Exegesis of 1 Peter, Its Situation and Strategy* (Philadelphia: Fortress Press, 1981), 87, 272; "Peter, First Epistle of," ABD vol. 5, 269–278, ed. David Noel Freedman (New York: Doubleday, 1992), 277.

11. Elliott, "Peter, First Epistle of," 270, 277.

12. Paul J. Achtemeier, *1 Peter,* Hermeneia (Minneapolis, MN: Fortress Press, 1996), 41–43, 48–50.

13. Hunter, "The First Epistle of Peter," 80–81, 87, 89; Fitzmyer, "The First Epistle of Peter," 362–363; Pheme Perkins, *First and Second Peter, James, and Jude* (Louisville, KY: John Knox Press, 1995), 14–15.

14. Unnik, "Peter, First Letter of," 761–762, 764.

15. Scot McKnight, *1 Peter,* NIVAC (Grand Rapids, MI: Zondervan, 1996), 23–24; Selwyn, *The First Epistle of St. Peter,* 44; Elliott, "Peter, First Epistle of," 273.

16. Elliott, *A Home for the Homeless,* 11, 23, 25, 35–36, 67–70, 131–132; quotation 11; "Peter, First Epistle of," 269.

17. Achtemeier, *1 Peter,* 56, 69–72, 80, 173–175; quotation 69; for the linguistic use of "aliens and strangers" cf. 56, n574.

18. Hunter, "The First Epistle of Peter," 112.

19. Unnik, "Peter, First Letter of," 762.

20. C. F. D. Moule, "The Nature and Purpose of I Peter," NTS 3 (1956–57):8; Selwyn, *The First Epistle of St. Peter,* 54–55; Fitzmyer, "The First Epistle of Peter," 362–363; Claude H. Thompson, "The First Letter of Peter," IOVCB, ed. Charles M. Laymon, 924–930 (Nashville and New York: Abingdon Press, 1971), 924; George Eldon Ladd, *A Theology of the New Testament* (Grand Rapids, MI: William B. Eerdmans, 1974), 594; Elliott, *A Home for the Homeless,* 23, 25, 67–70, 80; Pheme Perkins, *First and Second Peter, James, and Jude,* 15–16; Achtemeier, 1 Peter, 28–36.

21. (Emil) Richard Perdelwitz, *Die Mysterienreligion und das Problem des I. Petrusbriefes,* RVV 11/3 (Giessen: Alfred Toepelmann, 1911), 16–22.

22. Wilhelm Bornemann, "Der erste Petrusbrief—eine Taufrede des Silvanus?" ZNW 19 (1919–20):146–162.

23. Hans Windisch, *Die katholischen Briefe,* 3rd ed., ed. H. Preisker, HNT (Tübingen: J. C. B. Mohr [Paul Siebeck], 1951), 55, 73, 82.

24. Herbert Preisker, in Windisch, ibid., 157–160.

25. Frank L. Cross, *1 Peter: A Paschal Liturgy* (London: A. R. Mowbray, 1954), 28, 33–34, 37–41.

26. Marie-Emile Boismard, "Une liturgie baptismale dans la Prima Petri," RB 63 (1956): 185–189, 197–200; Selwyn, *The First Epistle of St. Peter, 62;* Thompson, "The First Letter of Peter," 924.

27. Moule, "The Nature and Purpose of I Peter," 4–6.

28. T. C. G. Thornton, "I Peter: A Paschal Liturgy?" JTS 12 (1961): 18–20, 25.

29. Thomas W. Leahy, "Peter, Epistles of St.," NCE vol. 11, 231–233 (New York: McGraw-Hill, 1967), 232; Elliott, *A Home for the Homeless,* 138; idem, "Peter, First Epistle of," 270–271; R. A. Martin, James, in R. A. Martin and John H. Elliott, *James/I–II Peter/Jude,* ACNT (Minneapolis, MN: Augsburg, 1982), 58.

30. Hunter, "The First Epistle of Peter," 112.

31. Elliott, *A Home for the Homeless,* 23, 25, 67–70, 80.

32. Ibid., 111, 115, 117–118, 148–149.

33. Ibid., 111–112, 115, 140, 231.

34. Ibid., 181, 189, 200–201; quotation 181.

35. David L. Balch, *Let Wives Be Submissive: The Domestic Code in 1 Peter,* SBLMS 26 (Chico, CA: Scholars Press, 1981), 88.

36. Ibid., 88, 95, 106, 118–119.

37. John H. Elliott, "1 Peter: Its Situation and Strategy: A Discussion with David Balch," in *Perspectives on First Peter,* NABPRSSS 9, ed. Charles H. Talbert, 61–78 (Macon, GA: Mercer University Press, 1986), 64–65, 70–72.

38. David L. Balch, "Hellenization/Acculturation in 1 Peter," in *Perspectives on First Peter,* NABPRSSS 9, ed. Charles H. Talbert, 79–101 (Macon, GA: Mercer University Press, 1986), 83–87, 93–100.

39. Perkins, *First and Second Peter, James, and Jude,* 41, 51.

40. Bartlett, "The First Letter of Peter," 271.

41. Goppelt, *A Commentary on 1 Peter,* 19–22.

42. Achtemeier, 1 Peter, 38, 69–72, 80, 173–175.

43. Bartlett, "The First Letter of Peter," 241.

44. Bo Reicke, *The Disobedient Spirits and Christian Baptism: A Study of 1 Pet. III.19 and Its Context,* ASNP 13 (Copenhagen: Ejnar Munksgaard, 1946), 56–59, 115–118.

45. Ibid., 118–125.

46. Ibid., 130–141.

47. Ibid., 132–133, 204–210.

48. Windisch, *Die katholischen Briefe,* 70–71; Hunter, "The First Epistle of Peter," 132–133; quotation 133; Hillyer, *1 and 2 Peter, Jude,* 112–124.

49. William Joseph Dalton, *Christ's Proclamation to the Spirits: A Study of 1 Peter 3:18—4:6,* AnBib 23 (Rome: Pontifical Biblical Institute, 1965), 124–162.

50. Ibid., 2nd ed., 1989:25–26, 105, 117–119; quotation 25–26.

51. Ibid., 1st ed., 1965:14.

52. Ibid., 1st ed., 1965:85; 2nd ed., 1989:105.

53. Selwyn, *The First Epistle of St. Peter,* 314–362; Fitzmyer, "The First Epistle of Peter," 367; Elliott, *I–II Peter/Jude,* in R. A. Martin and John H. Elliott, *James/I–II Peter/Jude,* 99, 101; Achtemeier, *1 Peter,* 245–256, 290–291; Bartlett, "The First Letter of Peter," 293–294.

3. 2 Peter

1. Albert E. Barnett, "The Second Epistle of Peter," IB vol. 12, 161–206 (New York and Nashville: Abingdon Press, 1957), 164.

2. J. Christiaan Beker, "Peter, Second Letter of," IDB vol. K-Q, ed. George A. Buttrick et al., 767–771 (New York and Nashville: Abingdon Press, 1962), 767–769.

3. Bo Reicke, *The Epistles of James, Peter, and Jude,* AB vol. 37 (Garden City, NY: Doubleday, 1964), 144–145.

4. Thomas W. Leahy, "The Second Epistle of Peter," JBC, ed. Raymond E. Brown, Joseph A. Fitzmyer, and Roland E. Murphy, 494–498 (Englewood Cliffs, NJ: Prentice-Hall, 1968), 494.

5. Claude H. Thompson, "The Second Letter of Peter," IOVCB, ed. Charles M. Laymon, 931–934 (Nashville and New York: Abingdon Press, 1971), 931.

6. Richard J. Bauckham, *Jude, 2 Peter,* WBC vol. 50 (Waco, TX: Word, 1983), 146–147, 160–161.

7. John H. Elliott, "Peter, Second Epistle of," ABD vol. 5, 282–287, ed. David Noel Freedman (New York: Doubleday, 1992), 283.

8. Pheme Perkins, *First and Second Peter, James, and Jude* (Louisville, KY: John Knox Press, 1995), 160–161.

9. Duane F. Watson, "The Second Letter of Peter," NIB vol. 12, 321–361 (Nashville: Abingdon Press, 1998), 323–324.

10. Norman Hillyer, *1 and 2 Peter, Jude,* NIBC (Peabody, MA: Hendrickson, 1992), 9–14, 214–215.

11. Leahy, "The Second Epistle of Peter," 495.

12. Richard J. Bauckham, "Jude, Epistle of," ABD vol. 3, 1098–1103, ed. David Noel Freedman (New York: Doubleday, 1992), 1100.

13. Beker, "Peter, Second Letter of," 768.

14. Barnett, "The Second Epistle of Peter," 164; John H. Elliott, *I–II Peter/Jude,* in R. A. Martin and John H. Elliott, *James/I–II Peter/Jude,* ACNT (Minneapolis, MN: Augsburg, 1982), 124; Jerome Neyrey, *2 Peter, Jude,* AB vol. 37C (New York: Doubleday, 1993), 121–122; Perkins, *First and Second Peter, James, and Jude,* 160; Watson, "The Second Letter of Peter," 328.

15. Cf. Elliott, "Peter, Second Epistle of," 284.

16. Reicke, *The Epistles of James, Peter, and Jude,* 148, 189–190; quotation 148; Hillyer, *1 and 2 Peter, Jude,* 13–14.

17. Cf. Elliott, who believes that the similarities between the two letters argue against the theory of a common source and for 2 Peter's use of Jude ("Peter, Second Epistle of," 284). Bauckham questions the assumption that the use of a common source can explain more clearly the differences between the two writings (*Jude, 2 Peter,* 142).

18. Bauckham, *Jude, 2 Peter,* 141, 260.

19. Barnett, "The Second Epistle of Peter," 164.

20. Elliott, "Peter, Second Epistle of," 287; cf. Watson, "The Second Letter of Peter," 325.

21. Neyrey, *2 Peter, Jude,* 128–132.

22. Reicke, *The Epistles of James, Peter, and Jude,* 160–162, 167–168.

23. Elliott, "Peter, Second Epistle of," 285; Neyrey, *2 Peter, Jude,* 135.

24. Barnett, "The Second Epistle of Peter," 164; Thompson, "The Second Letter of Peter," 931; Leahy, "The Second Epistle of Peter," 494; George Eldon Ladd, *A Theology of the New Testament* (Grand Rapids, MI: William B. Eerdmans, 1974), 602.

25. Bauckham, *Jude, 2 Peter,* 155–156.

26. Elliott, "Peter, Second Epistle of," 285–286; Jerome H. Neyrey, "The Form and Background of the Polemic in 2 Peter," JBL 99 (1980): 407–414; references to 2 Peter, 414–423; *2 Peter, Jude,* 112–113, 122–128.

27. Perkins, *First and Second Peter, James, and Jude,* 162, 174.

28. Elliott, "Peter, Second Epistle of," 284.

29. Reicke, *The Epistles of James, Peter, and Jude,* 146; Elliott, "Peter, Second Epistle of," 283; Bauckham, *Jude, 2 Peter,* 131–135.

30. Watson, "The Second Letter of Peter," 327.

31. Ibid., 335–336, 341, 350, 359; cf. also Neyrey, *2 Peter, Jude,* 112–118.

32. Frederick W. Danker, "2 Peter 1: A Solemn Decree," CBQ 40 (1978): 80.

33. Ernst Kaesemann, "An Apologia for Primitive Christian Eschatology," in *Essays on New Testament Themes,* 169–195, SBT vol. 41 (London: SCM Press, 1964), 169.

34. Ibid., 174–175, 179–180, 184, 190.

116   *What Are They Saying About the Catholic Epistles?*

35. Bauckham, *Jude, 2 Peter,* 151–153; Watson, "The Second Letter of Peter," 326–327.

36. Neyrey, "The Form and Background of the Polemic in 2 Peter," 430.

37. Ladd, *A Theology of the New Testament,* 603–604; quotation 603 n4.

38. Elliott, "Peter, Second Epistle of," 287.

4. 1 John

1. Amos N. Wilder, "The First, Second, and Third Epistles of John," IB vol. 12, 207–313 (New York and Nashville: Abingdon Press, 1957), 209, 215.

2. Ibid., 214–215, 227–229, 253.

3. George B. Caird, "John, Letters of," IDB vol. E-J, ed. George A. Buttrick et al., pp. 946–952 (New York and Nashville: Abingdon Press, 1962), 951–952.

4. Bruce Vawter, "The Johannine Epistles," JBC, ed. Raymond E. Brown, Joseph A. Fitzmyer, and Roland E. Murphy, 404–413 (Englewood Cliffs, NJ: Prentice-Hall, 1968), 405.

5. Massey H. Shepherd, "The First Letter of John," IOVCB, ed. Charles M. Laymon, 935–939 (Nashville and New York: Abingdon Press, 1971), 935; Pheme Perkins, *The Johannine Epistles,* NTM vol. 21 (Wilmington, DE: Michael Glazier, 1979), xiii–xiv; 76.

6. Rudolf Bultmann, *The Johannine Epistles: A Commentary on the Johannine Epistles,* ed. Robert W. Funk, Hermeneia (Philadelphia: Fortress Press, 1973), 1.

7. Raymond E. Brown, *The Epistles of John,* AB vol. 30 (Garden City, NY: Doubleday, 1982), 29.

8. Ibid.

9. Ibid., 30n71; 32n76.

10. Ibid., 30.

11. Ibid., 32, 101–102.

12. Robert Kysar, "John, Epistles of," ABD vol. 3, 900–912, ed. David Noel Freedman et al. (New York: Doubleday, 1992), 907.

13. Ibid., 907–908.

14. Ibid., 908–909; quotation 909.

15. Ibid., 909.

16. D. Moody Smith, *First, Second, and Third John* (Louisville, KY: John Knox Press, 1991), 14–15; Rudolf Schnackenburg, *The Johannine Epistles: Introduction and Commentary,* trans. Reginald and Ilse Fuller (New York: Crossroad, 1992), 38, 41, 55; Georg Strecker, *The Johannine Letters: A Commentary on 1, 2, and 3 John,* trans. Linda M. Maloney, ed. Harold Attridge, Hermeneia (Minneapolis, MN: Fortress, 1996), xxxvii, xl–xlii; C. Clifton Black, "The First, Second, and Third Letters of John," NIB vol. 12, 363–469 (Nashville: Abingdon Press, 1998), 365–368.

17. Ernst von Dobschuetz, "Johanneische Studien. I.," ZNW 8 (1907): 4.

18. Ibid., 4, 7–8.

19. Rudolf Bultmann, "Analyse des ersten Johannesbriefes," *Festgabe fuer Adolf Juelicher,* 138–158 (Tübingen: J. C. B. Mohr [Paul Siebeck], 1927), 138, 157–158.

20. Ibid., 156–157.

21. Ibid., 142–145, 147, 149.

22. Bultmann, *The Johannine Epistles,* 17–18, 45, 65, 76, 83.

23. Rudolf Bultmann, "Die kirchliche Redaktion des ersten Johannesbriefes," in *In Memoriam Ernst Lohmeyer,* ed. Werner Schmauch, 189–201 (Stuttgart: Evangelisches Verlagswerk, 1951); reprinted in *Exegetica: Aufsaetze zur Erforschung des Neuen Testaments,* ed. Erich Dinkler, 381–393 (Tübingen: J. C. B. Mohr [Paul Siebeck], 1967), 384–385, 388–393. (References here are to the 1967 reprint.)

24. Wilder, "The First, Second, and Third Epistles of John," e.g., 212, 221, 225, 251, 257, 262, 276.

25. Brown, *The Epistles of John,* 37–41.

26. Ibid., 42, 47.

27. Schnackenburg, *The Johannine Epistles,* 14–15.

28. Perkins, *The Johannine Epistles,* xvii–xviii, 68; quotations xvii, xviii.

29. Strecker, *The Johannine Letters,* 78.

30. Brown, *The Epistles of John,* 51–54, 76–77.

31. Cf. Caird, "John, Letters of," 947.

32. Brown, *The Epistles of John,* 67.

33. Kysar, "John, Epistles of," 905.

34. Schnackenburg, *The Johannine Epistles,* 17–18; quotation 18.

35. Ibid., 20–21; 21nn60–61.

36. The following interpreters see the false teachers as influenced in some way by the views of Cerinthus, although they do not claim that these teachers were actually disciples or associates of Cerinthus: Caird, "John, Letters of," 947; Vawter, "The Johannine Epistles," 410; Shepherd, "The First Letter of John," 936; Bultmann, *The Johannine Epistles,* 38n17; William Barclay, *The Letters of John and Jude,* DSBS (Louisville, KY: Westminster John Knox Press, 1976), 6; Strecker, *The Johannine Letters,* 76.

37. Wilder, "The First, Second, and Third Epistles of John," 211, 215.

38. Ibid., 209–210.

39. Shepherd, "The First Letter of John," 936.

40. Bultmann, *The Johannine Epistles,* 2–3, 43–44, 69.

41. Perkins, *The Johannine Epistles,* xix; 86–87.

42. Brown, *The Epistles of John,* 124–129, especially 126n296.

43. Kysar, "John, Epistles of," 902, 904–905.

44. Strecker, *The Johannine Letters,* xliii–xliv, 3, 78.

45. Ibid., xxix–xxx, xxiv.

46. Cf. Caird, "John, Letters of," 952.

47. Ibid.

48. Schnackenburg, *The Johannine Epistles,* 42–46; Strecker, *The Johannine Letters,* 188–191.

49. Barclay, *The Letters of John and Jude,* 81; cf. 121–122.

50. Perkins, *The Johannine Epistles,* 4–5, 11–12, 14, 25–28.

51. Ibid., 39–42; quotation 40.

52. Smith, *First, Second, and Third John,* 82–87; quotation 87.

53. Wilder, "The First, Second, and Third Epistles of John," 215; Vawter, "The Johannine Epistles," 405; Brown, *The Epistles of John,* 27–28; Kysar, "John, Epistles of," 911.

54. Bultmann, "Die kirchliche Redaktion des ersten Johannesbriefes," 388–391.

55. Bultmann, *The Johannine Epistles,* 17.

56. Guenter Klein, "'Das wahre Licht scheint schon': Beobachtungen zur Zeit und Geschichtserfahrung einer urchristlichen Schule," ZTK 68 (1971): 275.

57. Ibid., 277, 282.
58. Brown, *The Epistles of John,* 35 and 35n84.
59. Kysar, "John, Epistles of," 911.
60. Ibid., 908–909; quotation 909.
61. C. Clifton Black, "The Johannine Epistles and the Question of Early Catholicism," NovT 28 (1986): 132.
62. Ibid., 155.
63. Ibid.
64. Ibid., 156.
65. Ibid., 157–158.
66. Wilder, "The First, Second, and Third Epistles of John," 209.
67. Caird, "John, Letters of," 949.
68. Bultmann, *The Johannine Epistles,* 68.
69. Brown, *The Epistles of John,* 75–76.
70. Kysar, "John, Epistles of," 911–912.

5. 2 John

1. Eusebius, *The Ecclesiastical History,* vol. 1, trans. Kirsopp Lake (London: William Heinemann, and Cambridge, MA: Harvard University Press, 1959), 292–293. The reference is to 3.39.4.

2. Cf. William R. Schoedel, "Papias," ABD vol. 5, 140–142, ed. David Noel Freedman et al. (New York: Doubleday, 1992), 141. Schoedel discusses these possibilities without making a definite choice between them.

3. William Barclay, *The Letters of John and Jude,* DSBS (Louisville, KY: Westminster John Knox Press, 1976), 128–129.

4. Amos N. Wilder, "The First, Second, and Third Epistles of John," IB vol. 12, 207–313 (New York and Nashville: Abingdon Press, 1957), 303.

5. Ibid.

6. Barclay, *The Letters of John and Jude,* 127.

7. Rudolf Bultmann, *The Johannine Epistles: A Commentary on the Johannine Epistles,* ed. Robert W. Funk, Hermeneia (Philadelphia: Fortress Press, 1973), 95.

8. Rudolf Schnackenburg, *The Johannine Epistles: Introduction and Commentary,* trans. Reginald and Ilsa Fuller (New York: Crossroad, 1992), 277n.37.

9. Raymond E. Brown, *The Epistles of John*, AB vol. 30 (Garden City, NY: Doubleday, 1982), 648.

10. Robert Kysar, "John, Epistles of," ABD vol. 3, 900–912, ed. David Noel Freedman et al. (New York: Doubleday, 1992), 907–910.

11. Georg Strecker, *The Johannine Letters: A Commentary on 1, 2, and 3 John,* ed. Harold Attridge, Hermeneia (Minneapolis, MN: Fortress, 1996), 219.

12. Wilder, "The First, Second, and Third Epistles of John," 303.

13. Brown, *The Epistles of John,* 650–651, 679–680; quotation 650.

14. Schnackenburg, *The Johannine Epistles,* 273.

15. Wilder, "The First, Second, and Third Epistles of John," 210; Barclay, *The Letters of John and Jude,* 131, 135; Kysar, "John, Epistles of," 906.

16. Wilder, "The First, Second, and Third Epistles of John," 303.

17. Barclay, *The Letters of John and Jude,* 129–131.

18. Pheme Perkins, *The Johannine Epistles,* NTM vol. 21 (Wilmington, DE: Michael Glazier, 1979), 76.

19. Kysar, "John, Epistles of," 906.

20. Bultmann, *The Johannine Epistles,* 107.

21. Schnackenburg, *The Johannine Epistles,* 267.

22. Kysar, "John, Epistles of," 903–905.

23. Schnackenburg, *The Johannine Epistles,* 277–278.

24. Ibid., 276.

25. Bultmann, *The Johannine Epistles,* 110.

26. Wilder, "The First, Second, and Third Epistles of John," 304–305; quotation 305.

27. Kysar, "John, Epistles of," 909.

28. Wilder, "The First, Second, and Third Epistles of John," 306.

29. C. Clifton Black, "The First, Second, and Third Letters of John," NIB vol. 12, 363–469 (Nashville: Abingdon Press, 1998), 454.

30. Schnackenburg, *The Johannine Epistles,* 273.

31. Kysar, "John, Epistles of," 909.

32. Strecker, *The Johannine Letters,* 245, 249; quotation 249.

6. 3 John

1. C. Clifton Black, "The First, Second, and Third Letters of John," NIB vol. 12, 363–469 (Nashville: Abingdon Press, 1998), 459.

2. Amos N. Wilder, "The First, Second, and Third Epistles of John," IB vol. 12, 207–313 (New York and Nashville: Abingdon Press, 1957), 209–210, 308–312.

3. Rudolf Schnackenburg, *The Johannine Epistles: Introduction and Commentary*, trans. Reginald and Ilse Fuller (New York: Crossroad, 1992), 290.

4. William Barclay, *The Letters of John and Jude,* DSBS (Louisville, KY: Westminster John Knox Press, 1976), 136.

5. Wilder, "The First, Second, and Third Epistles of John," 95; Rudolf Bultmann, *The Johannine Epistles: A Commentary on the Johannine Epistles,* ed. Robert W. Funk, Hermeneia (Philadelphia: Fortress Press, 1973), 95; Black, "The First, Second, and Third Letters of John," 460.

6. Wilder, "The First, Second, and Third Epistles of John," 310–311.

7. Bultmann, *The Johannine Epistles,* 95; Robert Kysar, "John, Epistles of," ABD vol. 3, 900–912, ed. David Noel Freedman (New York: Doubleday, 1992), 906; Schnackenburg, *The Johannine Epistles,* 297–299.

8. Schnackenburg, *The Johannine Epistles,* 297–299.

9. Black, "The First, Second, and Third Letters of John," 467.

10. Wilder, "The First, Second, and Third Epistles of John," 311.

11. Barclay, *The Letters of John and Jude,* 136.

12. Pheme Perkins, *The Johannine Epistles,* NTM vol. 21 (Wilmington, DE: Michael Glazier, 1979), 76–77, 97–98.

13. Schnackenburg, *The Johannine Epistles,* 299.

14. Perkins, *The Johannine Epistles,* 76–77, 97–98; Bultmann, *The Johannine Epistles,* 100.

15. Wilder, "The First, Second, and Third Epistles of John," 209–210; 322.

16. Black, "The First, Second, and Third Letters of John," 464.

17. Kysar, "John, Epistles of," 906.

18. Schnackenburg, *The Johannine Epistles,* 300.

19. Georg Strecker, *The Johannine Letters: A Commentary on 1, 2, and 3 John,* ed. Harold Attridge, Hermeneia (Minneapolis, MN: Fortress, 1996), 256.

20. Black, "The First, Second, and Third Letters of John," 465.

21. Kysar, "John, Epistles of," 905.

22. Schnackenburg, *The Johannine Epistles,* 290–301.

23. Black, "The First, Second, and Third Letters of John," 459.

24. Kysar, "John, Epistles of," 908–909.

25. Strecker, *The Johannine Letters,* 248–249; quotation 249.

26. Black, "The First, Second, and Third Letters of John," 461. For a similar study of 1 John, see J. B. van der Watt, "Ethics in First John: A Literary and Socioscientific Perspective," CBQ 61 (1999): 491–511.

7. Jude

1. Thomas W. Leahy, "Jude, Epistles of St.," NCE vol. 8, 17–18 (New York: McGraw-Hill, 1967), 17.

2. Ibid.

3. Norman Hillyer, *1 and 2 Peter, Jude,* NIBC (Peabody, MA: Hendrickson, 1992), 17.

4. Richard J. Bauckham, *Jude, 2 Peter,* WBC vol. 50 (Waco, TX: Word, 1983), 11–13; "Jude, Epistle of," ABD vol. 3, 1098–1103, ed. David Noel Freedman (New York: Doubleday, 1992), 1100–1102. Cf. also Duane F. Watson, "The Letter of Jude," NIB vol. 12, 471–500 (Nashville: Abingdon Press, 1998), 474, 476.

5. Albert E. Barnett, "The Epistle of Jude," IB vol. 12, 315–343 (New York and Nashville: Abingdon Press, 1957), 317–318.

6. J. Christiaan Beker, "Jude, Letter of," IDB vol. E-U, ed. George A. Buttrick et al., 1009–1011 (New York and Nashville: Abingdon Press, 1962), 1010–1011; Thomas W. Leahy, "The Epistle of Jude," JBC, ed. Raymond E. Brown, Joseph A. Fitzmyer, and Roland E. Murphy, 378–380 (Englewood Cliffs, NJ: Prentice-Hall, 1968), 379; Claude H. Thompson, "The Book of Jude," IOVCB, ed. Charles M. Laymon, 942–944 (Nashville and New York: Abingdon Press, 1971), 942; Jerome Neyrey, 2 Peter, Jude, AB vol. 37C (New York: Doubleday, 1993), 33; Pheme Perkins, *First and Second Peter, James, and Jude* (Louisville, KY: John Knox Press, 1995), 142–143; Pierre Reymond, "Jude," IBC,

ed. William R. Farmer et al., 1838–1842 (Collegeville, MN: The Liturgical Press, 1998), 1838.

7. John H. Elliott, *I–II Peter/Jude,* in R. A. Martin and John H. Elliott, *James/I–II Peter/Jude,* ACNT (Minneapolis, MN: Augsburg, 1982), 164–167.

8. Neyrey, 2 *Peter, Jude,* 33–35.

9. Bauckham, *Jude, 2 Peter,* 7–8.

10. Barnett, "The Epistle of Jude," 318–319.

11. Bo Reicke, *The Epistles of James, Peter, and Jude,* AB vol. 37 (Garden City, NY: Doubleday, 1964), xv–xvi, xxi–xxiv, 191–192.

12. Leahy, "The Epistle of Jude," 378–379; quotation 378.

13. Bauckham, "Jude, Epistle of," 1102.

14. Bauckham, *Jude, 2 Peter,* 16.

15. Watson, "The Letter of Jude," 475.

16. Bauckham, "Jude, Epistle of," 1100.

17. Bauckham, *Jude, 2 Peter,* 12.

18. Bauckham, "Jude, Epistle of," 1100–1101.

19. Watson, "The Letter of Jude," 475–476.

20. Barnett, "The Epistle of Jude," 325, 328.

21. Beker, "Jude, Letter of," 1010–1011.

22. William Barclay, *The Letters of John and Jude,* DSBS (Louisville, KY: Westminster John Knox Press, 1976), 163.

23. Barclay, *The Letters of John and Jude,* 165–166, 200–202; Reymond, "Jude," 1839, 1841.

24. Bauckham, *Jude, 2 Peter,* 3.

25. Bauckham, *Jude, 2 Peter,* 4–5; "Jude, Epistle of," 1098–1099.

26. Bauckham, "Jude, Epistle of," 1098.

27. Hillyer, *1 and 2 Peter, Jude,* 19; Watson, "The Letter of Jude," 478–479.

28. Watson, "The Letter of Jude," 477.

29. Ibid., 477–478, 484, 487, 496.

30. Leahy, "The Epistle of Jude," 379.

31. Bauckham, *Jude, 2 Peter,* 8–9, 32–33; "Jude, Epistle of," 1100; Watson, "The Letter of Jude," 476.

32. Barnett, "The Epistle of Jude," 319.

References

Achtemeier, Paul J. *1 Peter.* Hermeneia. Minneapolis, MN: Fortress, 1996.

Baker, William R. *Personal Speech-Ethics in the Epistle of James.* WUNT 2.68. Tübingen: J. C. B. Mohr [Paul Siebeck], 1995.

Balch, David L. "Hellenization/Acculturation in 1 Peter." In *Perspectives on First Peter,* ed. Charles H. Talbert, 79–101. Macon, GA: Mercer University Press, 1986.

————. *Let Wives Be Submissive: The Domestic Code in 1 Peter.* SBLMS 26. Chico, CA: Scholars Press, 1981.

Barclay, William. *The Letters of John and Jude,* rev. ed. DSBS. Louisville, KY: Westminster John Knox Press, 1976.

Barnett, Albert E. "The Epistle of Jude." In IB vol. 12, ed. George A. Buttrick et al., 315–343. New York and Nashville: Abingdon Press, 1957.

————. "James, Letter of." In IDB vol. E-J, ed. George A. Buttrick et al., 794–799. New York and Nashville: Abingdon Press, 1962.

————. "The Second Epistle of Peter." In IB vol. 12, ed. George A. Buttrick et al., 161–206. New York and Nashville: Abingdon Press, 1957.

Bartlett, David L. "The First Letter of Peter." In NIB vol. 12, ed. Leander E. Keck et al., 227–319. Nashville: Abingdon Press, 1998.

Bauckham, Richard J. "Jude, Epistle of." In ABD vol. 3, ed. David Noel Freedman et al., 1098–1103. New York: Doubleday, 1992.

————. *Jude, 2 Peter.* WBC 50. Waco, TX: Word, 1983.

Beker, J. Christiaan. "Jude, Letter of." In IDB vol. E-J, ed. George A. Buttrick et al., 1009–1011. New York and Nashville: Abingdon Press, 1962.

————. "Peter, Second Letter of." In IDB vol. K-Q, ed. George A. Buttrick et al., 767–771. New York and Nashville: Abingdon Press, 1962.

Black, C. Clifton. "The First, Second, and Third Letters of John." In NIB vol. 12, ed. Leander E. Keck et al., 363–469. Nashville: Abingdon Press, 1998.

————. "The Johannine Epistles and the Question of Early Catholicism." NovT 28 (1986): 131–158.

Boismard, Marie-Emile. "Une liturgie baptismale dans la Prima Petri." RB 63 (1956): 182–208; 64 (1957): 161–183.

Bornemann, Wilhelm. "Der erste Petrusbrief—eine Taufrede des Silvanus?" ZNW 19 (1919–20): 143–165.

Brown, Raymond E. *The Epistles of John.* AB vol. 30. Garden City, NY: Doubleday, 1982.

————. "John, Epistles of St." In NCE vol. 7, 1078–1080. New York: McGraw-Hill, 1967.

Bultmann, Rudolf. "Analyse des ersten Johannesbriefes." In *Festgabe fuer Adolf Juelicher,* 138–158. Tübingen: J. C. B. Mohr, 1927.

————. *The Johannine Epistles: A Commentary on the Johannine Epistles,* ed. Robert W. Funk. Hermeneia. Philadelphia: Fortress, 1973.

————. "Die kirchliche Redaktion des ersten Johannesbriefes." In *In Memoriam Ernst Lohmeyer,* ed. Werner Schmauch, 189–201. Stuttgart: Evangelisches Verlagswerk, 1951.

Caird, George B. "John, Letters of." In IDB vol. E-J, ed. George A. Buttrick et al., 946–952. New York and Nashville: Abingdon Press, 1962.

Cantinat, Jean. *Les Epitres de Saint Jacques et de Saint Jude.* Paris: Librairie Lecoffre, J. Gabalda et Cie., 1973.

Cross, Frank L. *1 Peter: A Paschal Liturgy.* London: A. R. Mowbray, 1954.

Dalton, William Joseph. *Christ's Proclamation to the Spirits: A Study of 1 Peter 3:18–4:6.* AnBib vol. 23. Rome: Pontifical Biblical Institute, 1965; 2nd ed., 1989.

Danker, Frederick W. "2 Peter 1: A Solemn Decree." CBQ 40 (1978): 64–82.

Davids, Peter H. *The Epistle of James.* NIGTC. Exeter: The Paternoster Press, 1982.

Dibelius, Martin. *James: A Commentary on the Epistle of James,* rev. H. Greeven, trans. M. A. Williams. Hermeneia. Philadelphia: Fortress, 1976.

Dobschuetz, Ernst von. "Johanneische Studien. I." ZNW 8 (1907): 1–8.

Easton, Burton Scott. "The Epistle of James." In IB vol. 12, ed. George A. Buttrick et al., 1–74. New York and Nashville: Abingdon Press, 1957.

Elliott, John H. "1 Peter: Its Situation and Strategy: A Discussion with David Balch." In *Perspectives on First Peter,* ed. Charles H. Talbert, 61–78. Macon, GA: Mercer University Press, 1986.

———. *I–II Peter/Jude.* In R. A. Martin and John H. Elliott, *James/I–II Peter/Jude.* ACNT. Minneapolis, MN: Augsburg, 1982.

———. *A Home for the Homeless: A Sociological Exegesis of 1 Peter, Its Situation and Strategy.* Philadelphia: Fortress, 1981.

———. "Peter, First Epistle of." In ABD vol. 5, ed. David Noel Freedman et al., 269–278. New York: Doubleday, 1992.

———. "Peter, Second Epistle of." In ABD vol. 5, ed. David Noel Freedman et al., 282–287. New York: Doubleday, 1992.

Eusebius. *The Ecclesiastical History,* Vol. I. Trans. Kirsopp Lake. London: William Heinemann, and Cambridge, MA: Harvard University Press, 1959.

Farkasfalvy, Denis. "2 Peter." In *The International Bible Commentary,* ed. William R. Farmer et al., 1814–1822. Collegeville, MN: The Liturgical Press, 1998.

Felder, Cain Hope. "James." In *The International Bible Commentary,* ed. William R. Farmer et al., 1786–1801. Collegeville, MN: The Liturgical Press, 1998.

Fitzmyer, Joseph A. "The First Epistle of Peter." In JBC, ed. Raymond E. Brown, Joseph A. Fitzmyer, and Roland E. Murphy, 362–368. Englewood Cliffs, NJ: Prentice-Hall, 1968.

———. "New Testament Epistles." In JBC, ed. Raymond E. Brown, Joseph A. Fitzmyer, and Roland E. Murphy, 223–226. Englewood Cliffs, NJ: Prentice-Hall, 1968.

Gabarron, Jose Cervantes. "1 Peter." In *The International Bible Commentary,* ed. William R. Farmer et al., 1802–1813. Collegeville, MN: The Liturgical Press, 1998.

Goppelt, Leonhard. *A Commentary on 1 Peter,* ed. Ferdinand Hahn, trans. and augmented John E. Alsup. Grand Rapids, MI: William B. Eerdmans, 1993.

Hillyer, Norman. *1 and 2 Peter, Jude.* NIBC. Peabody, MA: Hendrickson, 1992.

Hunter, Archibald M. "The First Epistle of Peter." In IB vol. 12, ed. George A. Buttrick, 75–159. New York and Nashville: Abingdon Press, 1957.

Johnson, Luke Timothy. *The Letter of James.* AB vol. 37A. New York: Doubleday, 1995.

———. "The Letter of James." In NIB vol. 12, ed. Leander E. Keck et al., 175–225. Nashville: Abingdon Press, 1998.

Kaesemann, Ernst. "An Apologia for Primitive Christian Eschatology." In *Essays on New Testament Themes,* 169–195. SBT vol. 41. London: SCM Press, 1964.

Klein, Guenter. "'Das wahre Licht scheint schon': Beobachtungen zur Zeit and Geschichtserfahrung einer urchristlichen Schule." ZTK 68 (1971): 261–326.

Kysar, Robert. *I, II, III John.* ACNT. Minneapolis, MN: Augsburg, 1986.

———. "John, Epistles of." In ABD vol. 3, ed. David Noel Freedman et al., 900–912. New York: Doubleday, 1992.

Ladd, George Eldon. *A Theology of the New Testament.* Grand Rapids, MI: William B. Eerdmans, 1974.

Laws, Sophie. "James, Epistle of." In ABD vol. 3, ed. David Noel Freedman et al., 621–628. New York: Doubleday, 1992.

Leahy, Thomas W. "The Epistle of James." In JBC, ed. Raymond E. Brown, Joseph A. Fitzmyer, and Roland E. Murphy, 369–377. Englewood Cliffs, NJ: Prentice-Hall, 1968.

———. "The Epistle of Jude." In JBC, ed. Raymond E. Brown, Joseph A. Fitzmyer, and Roland E. Murphy, 378–380. Englewood Cliffs, NJ: Prentice-Hall, 1968.

———. "James, Epistle of St." In NCE vol. 7, 816–817. New York: McGraw-Hill, 1967.

———. "Jude, Epistle of St." In NCE vol. 8, 17–18. New York: McGraw-Hill, 1967.

———. "Peter, Epistles of St." In NCE vol. 11, 231–233. New York: McGraw-Hill, 1967.

————. "The Second Epistle of Peter." In JBC, ed. Raymond E. Brown, Joseph A. Fitzmyer, and Roland E. Murphy, 494–498. Englewood Cliffs, NJ: Prentice-Hall, 1968.

Martin, R. A. *James*. In R. A. Martin and John H. Elliott, *James/I–II Peter/Jude*. ACNT. Minneapolis, MN: Augsburg, 1982.

McKnight, Scot. *1 Peter*. NIVAC. Grand Rapids, MI: Zondervan, 1996.

Meyer, Arnold. *Das Raetsel des Jacobusbriefes*. BZNW vol. 10. Giessen: Alfred Toepelmann, 1930.

Moo, Douglas J. *The Letter of James*. PNTC. Grand Rapids, MI/Cambridge, UK: William B. Eerdmans, 2000.

Moule, C. F. D. "The Nature and Purpose of I Peter." NTS 3 (1956–57): 1–11.

Mussner, Franz. *Der Jakobusbrief*. HTKNT vol. 13. Freiburg: Herder, 1964. 5th ed. 1987.

Neyrey, Jerome H. "The Apologetic Use of the Transfiguration in 2 Peter 1:16–21." CBQ 42 (1980): 504–519.

————. "The Form and Background of the Polemic in 2 Peter." JBL 99 (1980): 407–431.

————. *2 Peter, Jude*. AB vol. 37C. New York: Doubleday, 1993.

Perdelwitz, Richard. *Die Mysterienreligion und das Problem des I. Petrusbriefes*. RVV vol. 11.3. Giessen: Alfred Toepelmann, 1911.

Perdue, Leo G. "Parenesis and the Epistle of James." ZNW 72 (1981): 241–256.

Perkins, Pheme. *First and Second Peter, James, and Jude*. Louisville, KY: John Knox Press, 1995.

————. *The Johannine Epistles*. NTM vol. 21. Wilmington, DE: Michael Glazier, 1979.

Reicke, Bo. *The Disobedient Spirits and Christian Baptism: A Study of 1 Pet. III. 19 and its Context*. ASNU vol. 13. Copenhagen: Ejnar Munksgaard, 1946.

————. *The Epistles of James, Peter, and Jude*. AB vol. 37. Garden City, NY: Doubleday, 1964.

Reymond, Pierre. "Jude." In *The International Bible Commentary*, ed. William R. Farmer et al., 1838–1842. Collegeville, MN: The Liturgical Press, 1998.

Sanders, E. P. *Paul and Palestinian Judaism: A Comparison of Patterns of Religion*. Philadelphia: Fortress, 1977.

Scheef, Richard L., Jr. "The Letter of James." In IOVCB, ed. Charles M. Laymon, 916–923. Nashville and New York: Abingdon Press, 1971.

Schlatter, Adolf. *Der Brief des Jakobus,* 2nd ed. Stuttgart: Calwer Verlag, 1956.

Schnackenburg, Rudolf. *The Johannine Epistles: Introduction and Commentary,* trans. Reginald and Ilse Fuller. New York: Crossroad, 1992.

Schoedel, William R. "Papias." In ABD vol. 5, ed. David Noel Freedman et al., 140–142. New York: Doubleday, 1992.

Selwyn, Edward Gordon. *The First Epistle of St. Peter.* London: Macmillan, 1961.

Shepherd, Massey H., Jr. "The First Letter of John." In IOVCB, ed. Charles M. Laymon, 935–939. Nashville and New York: Abingdon Press, 1971.

Smith, D. Moody. *First, Second, and Third John.* Louisville, KY: John Knox Press, 1991.

Strecker, Georg. *The Johannine Letters: A Commentary on 1, 2, and 3 John,* ed. Harold Attridge. Hermeneia. Minneapolis, MN: Fortress, 1996.

Talbert, Charles H., ed. *Perspectives on First Peter.* NABPRSSS vol. 9. Macon, GA: Mercer University Press, 1986.

Thompson, Claude H. "The Book of Jude." In IOVCB, ed. Charles M. Laymon, 942–944. Nashville and New York: Abingdon Press, 1971.

———. "The First Letter of Peter." In IOVCB, ed. Charles M. Laymon, 924–930. Nashville and New York: Abingdon Press, 1971.

———. "The Second Letter of Peter." In IOVCB, ed. Charles M. Laymon, 931–934. Nashville and New York: Abingdon Press, 1971.

Thornton, T. C. G. "I Peter. A Paschal Liturgy?" JTS 12 (1961): 14–26.

Unnik, W. C. van. "Peter, First Letter of." In IDB vol. K-Q, ed. George A. Buttrick et al., 758–766. New York and Nashville: Abingdon Press, 1962.

Vawter, Bruce. "The Johannine Epistles." In JBC, ed. Raymond E. Brown, Joseph A. Fitzmyer, and Roland E. Murphy, 404–413. Englewood Cliffs, NJ: Prentice-Hall, 1968.

Via, Dan O., Jr. "The Right Strawy Epistle Reconsidered: A Study in Biblical Ethics and Hermeneutics." JR 49 (1969): 253–267.

Watson, Duane F. "Elect Lady." In ABD vol. 2, ed. David Noel Freed-
man et al., 433–434. New York: Doubleday, 1992.
———. "The Letter of Jude." In NIB vol. 12, ed. Leander E. Keck,
471–500. Nashville: Abingdon Press, 1998.
———. "The Second Letter of Peter." In NIB vol. 12, ed. Leander E.
Keck et al., 321–361. Nashville: Abingdon Press, 1998.
Webb, Robert L. "Epistles, Catholic." In ABD vol. 2, ed. David Noel
Freedman, 569–570. New York: Doubleday, 1992.
Wilder, Amos N. "The First, Second, and Third Epistles of John." In IB
vol. 12, ed. George A. Buttrick, 207–313. New York and
Nashville: Abingdon Press, 1957.
Windisch, Hans. *Die katholischen Briefe,* 2nd ed. HNT vol. 15. Tübin-
gen: J. C. B. Mohr [Paul Siebeck], 1930; 3rd ed. revised H.
Preisker, 1951.